8 Minutes in the MORNING® for a Perfect Body

8 Minutes in the MORNING® for a Perfect Body

Lose Up to 4 Inches in Less Than 4 Weeks— Guaranteed!

JORGE CRUISE®

The *N.Y. TIMES* BEST-SELLING AUTHOR with over 3 million online weight-loss clients

RODALE

To all my online clients at JorgeCruise.com who sent me thousands of e-mails requesting that I write this book to help them get that special advantage to sculpt a flat belly fast. Enjoy!

© 2009 by Jorge Cruise, Inc.

Printed in the United States of America
Rodale Inc. makes every effort to use acid-free ∞, recycled paper ♻.

Jorge Cruise, 2 Pounds a Week in 8 Minutes, 8 Minutes in the Morning, 8 Minute Moves, Eat Nutritionally, Not Emotionally, Active Rest Moves, Cruise Down Plate, Cruise Down, Cruise Moves The People Solution, and Eat Fat to Get Fit are registered trademarks owned by Jorge Cruise, Inc. and JorgeCruise.com.

Book design by Christopher Rhoads

Library of Congress Cataloging-in-Publication Data is on file with the publisher.

ISBN-13 978–1–4351–1225–4

2   4   6   8   10   9   7   5   3   1   special sales hardcover

We inspire and enable people to improve their lives and the world around them
For more of our products visit **rodalestore.com** or call 800-848-4735

Acknowledgments

First, I want to thank my 3 million (and growing) weight-loss clients at JorgeCruise.com whom I have had the privilege of coaching. Without all their feedback, insights, and support, the Jorge Cruise weight-control brand would not be the success it is today.

I also must thank Oprah Winfrey, the lady who launched my career. She invited me to be a guest on her show in Chicago and introduced me to two people whose lives had changed because of my Web site. I will never forget that day. From that moment on, I knew that the Internet was a powerful resource that could change people's lives and bodies.

Heather, my wife, whom I love so much. Thanks again, baby doll, for being my source of love, balance, relaxation, and fun. You have shown me what life is really about and how to enjoy it all. I love you with all my heart and soul.

To my mom, Gloria, who is my shining star in the sky that looks over me. To my dad, Mel, for being the man who inspired me by his original weight loss. To my sister, Marta, who shed over 30 pounds and is now helping the world with her books on dating, relationships, and love. To my grandma Maria for showing me that at 92 years young resistance training can also add years to your life! To my grandpa George and grandma Dorothy who both passed away from being overweight . . . I promise to never forget the lesson from your passing about how essential it is to master your health before it's too late. I love you all.

To Phyllis McClanahan, my personal assistant and right hand. Thank you for keeping me focused and organized. You are priceless! Lisa Sharkey, my friend who has a heart of gold. To Bruce Barlean and the whole Barlean's family. Thanks for everything. To my buddy and great friend, Jade Beutler, and his family. To Ben Gage and his extraordinary negotiation and legal skills. To all my friends at Guthy-Renker, HarperCollins, and Hay House. Thank you all so much!

A special big thank-you to Rodale Books for all their initial support with my 8 Minute books. In particular, Alisa Bauman for helping me convey my message, Kelly Schmidt for managing all the project details, Chris Rhoads for his extraordinary design skills, Jackie Dornblaser for getting me where I needed to go, and Stephanie Tade, who truly made this project possible. Also a special thank-you to Dana Bacher, Marc Jaffe, Steve Murphy, and the Rodale family.

To my stellar team at *Prevention* magazine for helping me get my weight-loss column out to 11 million readers each month. Rosemary Ellis, Michele Stanten, and Robin Shallow, you are all the best!

Jan Miller, my literary agent, and Michael Broussard, her right arm, thank you for connecting me to the top people in the literary world. Jan, you are a gem. I look forward to a lifetime of great weight-loss books with you.

And finally, to my extraordinary and magical public relations team: Cindy Ratzlaff and Cathy Gruhn at Rodale, Mary Lengle at Spotted Dog Communications, and Arielle Ford and Katherine Kellmeyer at the Ford Group in San Diego. Thank you all so much from the bottom of my heart for your hard work, time, and efforts! Thank you, thank you, thank you!

Contents

From the Desk of Jorge Cruise®

Dear Friend,

Welcome to my ALL-NEW *8 Minutes in the Morning for a Perfect Body* book! I want to congratulate you and thank you for selecting me to be your coach. Together we are about to embark on the adventure of a lifetime.

You are probably wondering how in the next 4 weeks you will lose up to 6 inches of belly fat or up to 4 inches from your hips and thighs in just 8 minutes a day. Well, the answer is that there is a revolution going on in the field of weight loss. Aerobics and dieting are out. And *resistance training* is in. Experts agree that the fastest way to lose weight is to build lean muscle tissue, which burns fat. The problem is that no one has time to work out.

Well, my *8 Minutes in the Morning for a Perfect Body* program has changed the rules. It will empower you to shed the belly fat and sculpt your hips and thighs at home and in just a few minutes a day.

So here's what I want you to do right now: First, read Part 1 of the book. It will show you how the program works. Once you are done reading those chapters, you will be ready to move on to Parts 2 and 3. There, you'll start losing up to 6 inches from your belly or up to 4 inches from your hips and thighs in less than 4 weeks—in just 8 minutes a day. Enjoy!

Your friend,

Jorge Cruise

America's #1 online weight-loss specialist
www.jorgecruise.com

Part 1

Your Perfect Body

Chapter 1

8 Minutes for a Perfect Body

Get Ready to Lose Up to 6 Inches of Belly Fat and 4 Inches from Your Hips and Thighs

make the commitment

Thank you for selecting me to be your weight-loss coach. I congratulate you for making the commitment to transform not only your belly but also your life!

I developed my *8 Minutes in the Morning for a Perfect Body* program with the feedback from millions of people just like you. Through my Web site, www.jorgecruise.com, I've had the honor of helping more than 3 million clients shed stubborn fat, end emotional eating, and take those first confident steps into new lives—lives that are full of possibility. I understand the struggle to lose weight

and keep it off. I've been there. I struggled with weight as a child and young man. I come from an overweight family. We struggled to slim down and shape up. It is that struggle that led me to my life's work.

That's why I'm so excited for you. You are about to start a transformation that will revolutionize your life and your body.

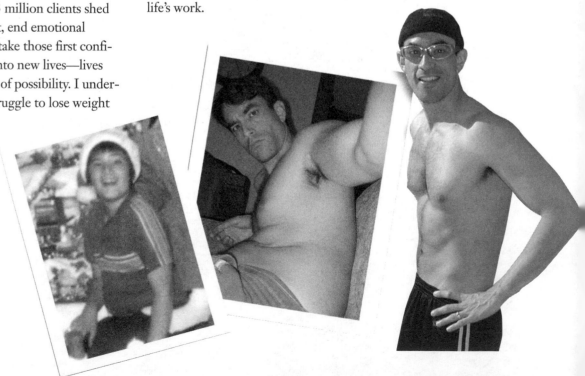

the 8 minute revolution

Now for the big question that you've probably been wondering since you picked up this book. How will you lose up to 6 inches from your belly and up to 4 inches from your hips and thighs in less than 4 weeks in just 8 minutes a day?

To understand the answer to that question, I must first let you in on a secret. You see, there's a revolution going on the field of weight loss. Cardiovascular exercise (otherwise known as aerobics) and dieting are out. Resistance training is in. Experts now agree that you must create lean muscle tissue in order to shed fat anywhere in your body, and particularly in your lower half. Lean muscle provides the

your "8 minute" edge

In just 8 minutes each morning, you will:

• Firm and tone your belly and thigh muscles

• Burn the fat that's hiding your beautiful body

• Lose up to 2 pounds of fat a week

• Shrink your waistline

• Improve your health

• Boost your confidence

key that opens the lock on even the most sluggish of metabolisms. Rev up your metabolism and you will burn calories all day long, incinerating the fat in your abdomen and hips and thighs that's hiding your beautiful body.

That's why all of my 8 Minutes in the Morning programs focus on building lean muscle tissue. You must exercise aerobically for a half-hour or more to burn the same number of calories as the 24/7 metabolism boost that you get from just 8 daily minutes of resistance training. If you've avoided exercise because you thought you didn't have time to work out, I'm happy to tell you that *8 Minutes in the Morning for a Perfect Body* changes the rules. In just 8 minutes each day, you will create the muscle needed to rev up your metabolism and incinerate the fat in your abdomen. No other weight-loss program provides such a big return on such a small investment. Take the 8-minute challenge. It's well worth the time!

tested by people just like you

Are you still wondering how I can promise you such extraordinary results in just 8 minutes a day?

Here's a little more background

on how I created this exciting program. As I said earlier, through my JorgeCruise.com online club, I have the privilege of working with 3 million online clients. And my online clients *don't* have time to waste. They are very busy people with full schedules. They want to lose weight in the most efficient and simple manner possible. Thus, "Weight Loss for Busy People" has become what the Jorge Cruise® brand is all about. I am 100 percent dedicated to helping time-challenged people lose weight and keep it off. That's my specialty.

And those very same clients helped me create and test the *8 Minutes in the Morning for a Perfect Body* program. You see, after the success of my *New York Times* best-selling books, more than 1 million new clients logged on to JorgeCruise.com and shared with me how they lost weight with my first two programs. They told me stories about how my first book, *8 Minutes in the Morning*, helped them lose 15 to 20 pounds or how they shed a stunning 30 or more pounds with my second book, *8 Minutes in the Morning for Real Shapes, Real Sizes*.

But many of them wanted more. They asked me to help them target specific trouble

robert sutherlin jr. shrunk 4 inches from his belly!

"Jorge's program is so easy to do and definitely targets the belly area. When I concentrate on keeping the muscles tight during the exercise, it is easy to get the 'burn' quickly, which, to me, means that I'm doing them correctly!

"To keep my eating in check, I do a lot of self-talk. Where once I would have simply turned to the fridge when I was feeling down, bored, or lonely, I now ask myself if I really want whatever it is I am planning to eat. I catch myself just looking through the fridge and I say to myself, 'Why are you eating? You're not hungry, so either get busy or go to bed.' It often helps me just close the fridge door and walk away."

Robert lost 19 pounds of belly fat.

zones. And the most requested areas were *the belly and hips and thighs.*

Well, I knew what I had to do. I designed an 8-minute program that specifically targets the lower half, and I tested it on my online clients over and over until I was completely confident that it would help *everyone* shed fat in just 8 minutes a day. This pro-gram builds on the success of my two other books. It takes the weight-loss formula that I've tested again and again on millions of clients and applies it specifi-cally to the belly area. I'm happy to tell you that anyone can use this supplementary program to beautify the body—in just 8 min-utes a day!

It doesn't matter whether you've lost weight with one of my other books or whether this is your first experience with a Jorge Cruise® program. Either way, you will experience fantastic results. If you haven't read my other books, that's okay. Every-thing you need to lose weight and firm up your body is right here within the pages of this book.

Chapter 2

The Jorge Cruise® Revolution

Discover the Fat-Burning Power of Creating Lean Muscle

a closer look at the program

As I told you in chapter 1, the number one secret to your perfect body is building lean muscle tissue. Lean muscle is what you need to boost your metabolism and burn the fat.

Every aspect of my *8 Minutes in the Morning for a Perfect Body* program focuses on that one important weight-loss principle. If you commit to creating lean muscle with me through this book, you will firm up your body, lose up to 6 inches in less than 4 weeks, and truly feel your confidence soar.

I'll explain more about how the program works very soon, but first, let's take a look at why you tend to gain fat in your belly and hips and thighs.

the science of body shaping

Too often I hear my clients beating themselves up over their body shapes. They call their bodies horrible names and berate themselves for their lack of willpower. I often tell them—

as I am telling you right now— that getting rid of the fat is *not* about willpower. In fact, if you use only willpower to try to whittle away that fat, you will almost always fight a losing battle.

Let me explain. To understand why willpower alone won't help you beautify your body, you must first understand why you tend to gain fat in your lower body in the first place. There are many reasons, but topping the list are your unique *genetics*. Everyone has a proliferation of fat cells in certain predictable body areas: the back of the upper arms, the belly, the thighs, breasts (in women), and the buttocks. In some people, fat cells in certain areas are more active than others, creating different-shaped bodies.

Genetically speaking, there are

two predominant body types. Some tend to gain fat in their lower bodies, creating what's known as a pear shape. And others tend to gain fat in their abdomens, creating what's known as an apple shape. If you're a genetic apple, your body will prefer to store fat in your abdomen and hips and thighs. Whenever you eat too much, the extra calories will go straight to these areas!

You can't change your genetics, but you can change your body shape. You'll soon learn how!

Here are some other factors that can influence whether your belly and hips and thighs rank as your number one trouble spots.

Pregnancy. When you're pregnant, your growing baby stretches out your abdominal muscles, weakening them and molding them into a outwardly rounded position. If your abdomen was already weak going into your pregnancy, your growing belly will bulge out sooner—as soon as 4 months— than someone who had strong abdominal muscles going into pregnancy. Strong abdominal muscles help to better hold the baby in position, preventing it from bulging outward as quickly.

After 9 months of pregnancy and subsequent childbirth, however, just about all women—no matter their pre-pregnancy fitness—are left with weak and flabby abdominal muscles. If you had a C-section, then your abdominal strength is almost zero because the surgery sliced through and consequently weak-ened your muscles. When your abdominal muscles are weak, they can't do as good a job of holding your internal organs in place. You end up with a belly bulge—even if you don't have much belly fat. But you can do something about this—no matter how many babies you've had.

Menopause. Generally, the female hormone estrogen tends to encourage fat storage in the buttocks, breasts, and thighs. That's because the body can more easily access fat in these areas to feed a growing fetus and to create milk for lactation. However, after menopause, estrogen levels drop, and fat storage starts to change. Many women notice that they begin to store fat in their bellies after menopause. Again, you can do something about it!

Are You a Pear or an Apple?

Where do you carry your weight? If you carry your weight around your arms, legs, and thighs, you're a pear shape. If your fat is in your abdominal area, you're what's known as an apple shape—and that could be a risk to your health, since abdominal fat prompts your liver to release its stored fatty acids, which raises your cholesterol levels. It also changes the levels of hormones that regulate your appetite and fat storage, so you feel hungry, eat more, and store more fat around your belly!

In addition, studies have shown that women who have larger waists (36 inches or more) are more likely to develop diabetes. Women whose waists were 32 inches or more were twice as likely to have a heart attack. Your chances for breast cancer, high blood pressure, back and joint pain, varicose veins, and overall fatigue are also much greater.

But you can prevent all of that by strength training with my special Cruise Moves, which have been designed to create lean muscle tissue and burn that belly fat!

The Apple

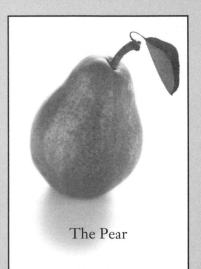

The Pear

Gender. Because of differing levels of sex hormones, men tend to store fat in their abdomens whereas women tend to store fat in their butts and legs. This isn't true in all people all the time. Genetics and menopause can override this tendency. So if you are a 30-year-old woman with an apple body shape, that doesn't mean there's anything wrong with you. It only means that your genetics are overriding your sex hormones, directing fat storage to your belly.

Metabolic syndrome. Long ago, when men and women survived by hunting and gathering, some people developed the tendency to store fat very easily and burn fat very slowly. Known as a "thrifty" set of genes, this tendency allowed our ancient ancestors to survive long famines. Women with the thrifty set of genes were able to get pregnant and breastfeed even when food was very scarce.

Today, probably about half of the population or more carries one or more of these thrifty genes. And though these genes may have allowed our ancient ancestors to thrive, they don't work well for us today. Our sedentary lifestyles coupled with abundant food make it easy for those with these thrifty genes to gain weight. In addition,

researchers believe that this set of genes tends to direct fat storage into the abdomen, which sets off that vicious cycle.

If you have the thrifty genes, your insulin levels tend to rise too high when you eat certain foods. Your pancreas secretes the hormone insulin to help shuttle sugar into cells. However, too much of this hormone spells trouble. Despite the fact that you just ate and don't need any more calories, the high levels of insulin can make you hungry (which makes you eat more) as well as cause enzymes in the liver to signal your body to store fat. Insulin tends to trigger fat storage particularly in the abdomen. Again, though these genes may make it harder for you to beautify your belly than someone who doesn't have them, it doesn't make it impossible. My program will help!

Stress. When you feel stressed, you set off your fight-or-flight response. This triggers the release of many stress hormones, notably cortisol. These hormones work to help you better handle your stressor. They speed up your heart rate, dilate your blood vessels, and shuttle blood away from your digestive track and to your muscles.

But it can work against you, too. The fight-or-flight response

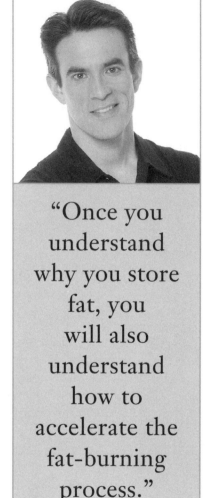

"Once you understand why you store fat, you will also understand how to accelerate the fat-burning process."

also tells your liver to make fuel available to be burned. The idea is that you will need energy to run or fight, so your liver makes sugar from its stored glycogen. You don't use this sugar because you didn't actually fight or flee, but your liver doesn't know that. So it triggers your brain to make you feel hungry. The calories you eat go straight to the fat cells in your tummy! If you trigger your fight-or-flight response chronically, your body will begin to try to store up as much fat as possible—creating an arsenal of stored calories to help you flee or fight.

The American lifestyle. As little as 100 years ago, Americans moved as a way of life. Our jobs required manual labor and we had to walk to most destinations. Today, however, we can accomplish just about every task while seated. We order food over the phone, shop online, and use the drive-through for just about everything. As a result, your abdominal muscles are hardly ever called into action. As they grow weaker, they fail to do their job of holding in your abdominal contents. Your internal organs begin to pooch outward. As your belly grows, it pulls your lower spine forward, which accentuates your belly bulge. But you can do something about this!

how lack of muscle accelerates fat gain

Now that you understand the factors that influence where you tend to gain fat, let's take a look at the most important reason fat tends to accumulate *anywhere* in the body.

This is where things get exciting. Once you understand why you store fat, you will also understand how to accelerate the fat-burning process. This will set you free!

I just told you about how the American lifestyle contributes to the apple body type. Now let's take a look at how it relates to fat storage. Your muscles need activity not only to grow, but also to maintain their size. Due to our sedentary lives, many of us lose a minimum of 5 pounds of muscle mass during each decade of life as early as age 15. This is disastrous to your resting metabolism.

Let me explain. Your muscles are metabolically active tissues that work hard 24 hours a day to maintain themselves. You probably think of your muscles as burning calories whenever you use them—such as during walking or yard work. But your muscles also burn calories when they are *not* moving, as they break down and recreate protein. That's why your lean muscle mass is so important to your success. Each pound of muscle in your body burns 50 calories a day—at rest.

If you lose 5 pounds of muscle a decade, by age 50 that means your metabolism may be burning 875 fewer calories a day. Each lost pound of muscle slows your metabolism by 50 calories a day!

You must reverse this trend with Cruise Moves, my unique resistance-training exercises that help create long, lean, supple muscle. On my program, you can expect to add 5 pounds or more of muscle, helping you to burn 250 or more extra calories a day!

Many people say to me, "But Jorge, I want to lose weight, not

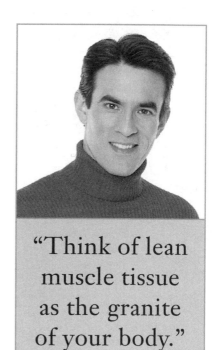

"Think of lean muscle tissue as the granite of your body."

gain it. Why would I want to add 5 pounds of muscle?" Here's another exciting benefit of lean muscle tissue. Lean muscle is very dense and compact, unlike fat tissue, which is soft and expansive. Think of lean muscle tissue as the granite of your body and fat as the cotton. A pound of granite takes up much less space than a pound of cotton, right? So even if you have an equal exchange of 1 pound of muscle for 1 pound of fat—and didn't lose any weight on the scale—you will still slim down in appearance. However, on the *8 Minutes in the Morning for a Perfect Body* program you will do better than an equal exchange. Each pound of lean muscle will burn off more

than a pound of fat, allowing you to lose 2 pounds a week, on average.

two myths exposed

There's a pervasive myth about resistance training that tends to cause some women to shy away from it. And it's simply not true! Many women tell me that they worry that resistance training will build bulky muscles similar to a man's. That's not true. First, women don't have the hormones to put on that type of muscle. Second, the specific nature of my Cruise Moves will help you to create long, lean, sleek, sexy muscles. The muscle tissue that you will be creating will *not* be bulky, but rather lean, long, and firm. It will look beautiful and best of all it will *burn belly and hip and thigh fat*!

Here's another myth that I often hear. Many people ask me, "Jorge, why should I also tone the muscles in my arms and legs when my belly is my trouble area?" They tell me that they've heard that it's best to burn belly fat by working *only* their belly muscles and not the rest of their bodies. For example, they do a half-hour of abdominal crunches a day—and nothing else. Well, I can tell

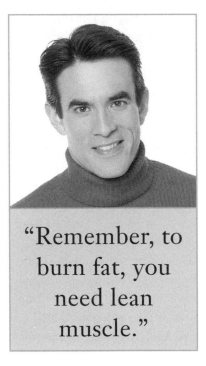

"Remember, to burn fat, you need lean muscle."

you that spot toning is a big myth. Fat burning just doesn't work this way.

Remember that lean muscle that I mentioned? Well, you need to create lean muscle all over your body to see true results. If you focus only on moves for your abdomen, you won't raise your metabolism enough to burn your belly fat. Only when you strengthen your entire body will you boost your metabolism enough to burn off the layer of fat that is hiding your beautiful abdominal muscles. You must burn off that fat to allow your abdominal muscles to show through!

your "8 minute" edge

The *8 Minutes in the Morning for a Perfect Body* program will help you to burn fat by building lean muscle. You'll do so in two steps:

Step 1:
8 Minutes
of Cruise Moves

Step 2:
Eating Nutritionally,
***Not* Emotionally**

In fact, in a study done at the University of Alabama, those who completed a total-body strengthening program—such as the program you will do in chapters 4 and 6—lost much more belly fat than those who did only abdominal exercises. Additional research shows that with just a few months of resistance training, you can experience a startling 7 percent increase in metabolic rate. That means you'll burn hundreds of extra calories a day!

Working muscles throughout your body will help create the muscle needed to burn the fat! In addition to boosting your metabolism, my total-body approach will also help create balanced strength and a more proportioned appearance. Often, when you focus on just strengthening one muscle group, you create strength imbalances that can lead to injuries. You must strengthen your entire body in order to remain fit and healthy—and beautiful.

a two-step approach

So remember, to burn fat, you need lean muscle. *Muscle* is what governs your metabolism.

The *8 Minutes in the Morning for a Perfect Body* program will help you create that important lean muscle tissue in two critical steps. The program works much like the process of building a new house. To build a house you would need someone to do the physical work. That person would then use important building materials to construct the house. In the *8 Minutes in the Morning for a Perfect Body* program, the exercises, or Cruise Moves, provide the physical work needed to create lean muscle. Just as hiring your contractor is the first step to building a house, committing to your Cruise Moves is your first step to building a beautiful body.

Your eating plan—the Cruise Down Plate—will provide your body with the building materials it needs to allow your muscles to grow. Just as buying the cement, 2 3 4s, and nails would be your second step to building a home, embarking on your eating plan is the second step to creating new lean muscle that will burn fat. You'll learn more about this important two-step process coming pages.

the magic of lean muscle

Let's take a closer look at the amazing power of lean muscle tissue, starting with how it affects your metabolism.

Many factors affect your metabolism, and some are beyond your control. For example, some people are genetically gifted with fast metabolisms. These are those enviable people who do everything wrong: They eat huge servings of fattening foods and seem to never lift a finger. Yet, they never seem to gain an ounce. It seems no matter how much they eat, they remain as slim as a rail.

On the other hand, some people are genetically cursed with a slow metabolism. A leftover from years ago when calories were scarce, such a slow metabolism was helpful during times of famine. When food was scarce, someone whose body burned fewer calories and conserved the most fat tended to survive the longest.

Unfortunately, a slow metabolism doesn't help you much today. Now we are surrounded by calories in the form of fast food, frozen dinners, and huge portions served up at restaurants. Food is abundant. And if you were genetically walloped with a slow metabolism, every stray calorie seems to make a beeline for your hips and thighs.

Your age and gender also affect your metabolism. Men tend to burn more calories throughout the day than women. And as we age, certain hormonal changes also tend to slow the metabolism.

It's true that you can't change your genetics or age. But that doesn't mean your battle against hip and thigh fat won't be won. All of us have a very powerful metabolic weapon at our disposal, one that we can change for the better.

That weapon is *lean muscle tissue*.

Unlike fat, muscle is metabolically active tissue. Each pound of lean muscle tissue burns 50 calories a day.

That's why lean muscle is so important to your metabolism. It's the key to turning up your

metabolic furnace and burning extra calories all day long.

the incredible shrinking muscle

Unfortunately, our lifestyles do not promote the creation or maintenance of lean muscle. Most of us sit during the vast majority of the day. We sit in our cars while on the way to work, and then sit at a desk. Thanks to modern conveniences such as seated lawn mowers, self-propelled vacuums, moving walkways, and escalators, we need not move much. The advent of the EZ-Pass system has eliminated the need to roll down our car windows and reach outside to hand change over to a toll attendant. Credit card readers have eliminated the need to walk from our car to an attendant in order to pay for gas at fill-up stations. Food at the grocery store comes pre-chopped, so we need not use muscles in our hands and arms to turn a carrot into carrot slices.

Each year, such labor-saving inventions become more and more prevalent—and we burn fewer calories as a result.

Due to lack of movement, our muscles tend to shrink with age.

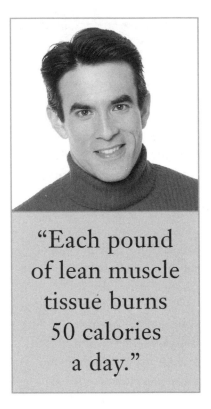

"Each pound of lean muscle tissue burns 50 calories a day."

After age 20, most people lose 5 pounds of muscle per decade. By age 50, that amounts to 750 fewer burned calories a day—the amount of calories many people eat for breakfast and lunch. No wonder most of us tend to gain weight as we age!

Many people respond to creeping weight gain with dieting. But this couldn't be any more counterproductive. When you crash diet, your body goes into a survival mode, turning down your metabolism and turning up your appetite. It also tries to preserve your fat tissue

---

your "8 minute" edge

On the *8 Minutes in the Morning for a Perfect Body* program you will build lean muscle, which will help you:

• Speed up your metabolism

• Burn more calories 24 hours a day

• Shrink the size of your hips and thighs

by burning up your muscle tissue! This couldn't be more detrimental to your metabolism. You may succeed in losing the weight, but as soon as you go off the diet, it comes back—and then some. Worst of all, each time you diet, you slow your metabolism more and more.

You must reverse this destructive process by creating new lean muscle tissue. It's the only way to rev up your metabolism and slim down your hips and thighs for good!

how the jorge cruise® formula builds muscle

So you see, lean muscle is the key to boosting your metabolism and burning fat.

Now, let's take a closer look at the best and most efficient way to create lean muscle: resistance training. Though cardiovascular activities such as running and walking maintain a certain amount of muscle, you'll get a much bigger bang for your buck with resistance training. And my targeted Cruise Moves will help you resistance train in the most efficient way possible.

Because of the way I've paired my Cruise Moves, you never need to rest during a session, so you never waste precious time between movements. Also, by working your muscles every day (with weekends off), you'll benefit from an exercise afterburn, boosting your metabolism

the spot-toning myth

You may have heard very respected experts say that you can't spot tone. They say that you must learn to accept the shape of your body just the way it is. They say that you cannot shrink one area of your body and not another.

Well, I'm happy to tell you that the spot-toning caution is only half-true. Here's the truth: If you focus only on your thighs, for example, by doing hundreds of leg lifts, you probably won't slim down. Moving just one area of your body over and over doesn't result in fat burning in that one spot.

However, if you target your entire body—upper, middle, and lower—with certain resistance-training moves, you can boost your metabolism high enough that your body burns fat all day long. This will help burn fat all over your body, including your thighs. Doing resistance-training moves for your upper body will help fill out your weak area, helping to balance your lower half. If you combine that with

a healthy eating plan, you *will* shed the fat.

It's true that the fat in your thighs is the most stubborn type of fat there is. But that doesn't mean you can't burn it. An exciting study done at the University of Maryland and published in the prestigious *American Journal of Clinical Nutrition* showed that exercise and a healthy diet resulted in a 15-pound weight loss after 6 months. Though that may not sound like a lot of weight on the scale, know that these women were not extremely overweight to start with. And here's the real exciting news. The women were able to shrink their thigh circumferences by 4 percent—the same amount as the rest of their bodies.

So, if you think that you lose weight everywhere else in your body first—and in your thighs last—it may only be that you focused too much on calorie restriction and not enough on creating the lean muscle needed to boost your metabolism.

a little more for the rest of the day after your sessions.

My program takes just *8 minutes a day* to complete and that's key. Many people can motivate themselves at the beginning of a weight-loss program to exercise for a half-hour or more. But that motivation usually wanes at some point. Does that sound familiar to you? Have you started and stopped fitness plans before?

In order to stick with a program, you must start a program that easily fits into your life. You might struggle to find 30 minutes a day to exercise, but how about 8 minutes? I bet you can do that! Cruise Moves are designed to give you exactly what you need and no more. They will help you to fill out your shoulders and slim down your thighs, creating a balanced appearance.

You'll learn more about why the program is so efficient in chapters 4 and 6.

In addition to 8 daily minutes of Cruise Moves, you will also get a delicious meal plan with essential muscle-making materials you'll need to create your new body. Remember: Dieting slows the metabolism and shrinks muscle tissue. But overeating can be just as destructive as dieting, particularly if you overeat to soothe negative emotions. My eating plan in chapter 3 will help you to avoid nutritional pitfalls. You'll learn how to eat nutritionally and *not emotionally*. You'll learn how to treat food as a tool for your body. Think of food as the tool that helps create lean muscle and boosts your metabolism.

a 2-step process

On the *8 Minutes in the Morning for a Perfect Body* program, you'll create lean muscle in two steps. Your first and most important step: 8 minutes of focused Cruise Moves each morning. These moves will create the lean muscle needed to boost your metabolism. They also will help to shape and tone your thighs, giving them a wonderful lean, enviable contour.

But to experience best results, you must combine your Cruise Moves with a second step: Eat Nutritionally, Not Emotionally. To create muscle, you must eat the materials to make muscle tissue. But you must not overeat then due to emotional stresses. If you overeat while doing your Cruise Moves, you'll hinder your success. Also, a healthy eating plan helps to support muscle growth and can also help boost your metabolism. You'll learn about this in the next chapter.

Chapter 3

Eat Nutritionally, *Not* Emotionally

your building materials

Now that you've hired the contractor (you) to do the physical work (the Cruise Moves) to create your perfect body, you are ready to learn about your second step to success. You are ready to use the building materials (the meal plan) needed to construct the sculpted body of your dreams.

Just as you could not build a house without wood and nails, you cannot create a toned body without proper nutrition. The second step to creating a beautiful body is just as important as the first, *so please don't try to save time by skipping it*. Your building materials (meal plan) will help you to create the lean muscle needed to burn the fat. Later in the chapter I will share with you some simple tips on how to overcome self-sabotage by eliminating emotional eating. You see, **emotional eating** can be the number one roadblock to keeping your body firm and flat.

your "8 minute" edge

The *8 Minutes in the Morning for a Perfect Body* eating plan is simple and easy. You will love it because it involves no banned foods, calorie counting, or starvation dieting! On this program, you will:

• Learn how to eat all your favorite foods in the correct portions

• Learn the difference between "nutritional eating" and "emotional eating"

• Fill your body with the right foods needed to build muscle and burn fat

how to eat nutritionally

Your eating plan will help you to maximize the foods that will support lean muscle tissue development and minimize the foods that support the growth of fat cells.

"The Cruise Down Plate will give you the ideal portion of protein to build lean muscles."

THE CRUISE DOWN PLATE®

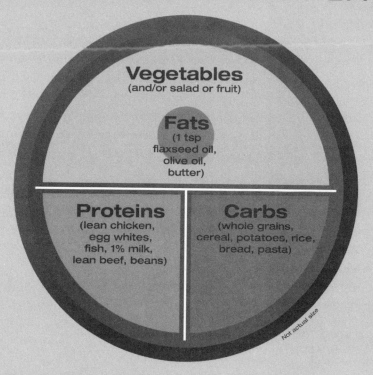

Follow one simple rule: Fill half of a standard 9-inch plate with vegetables and the other half with equal portions of carbohydrates and protein foods, along with a teaspoon of fat. It's that easy!

What's my eating secret? I call it my *Cruise Down Plate*. It will help you to simply and almost automatically eat the right foods in the right portions. In addition to helping you fuel muscle growth, the plate will help you burn fat in a few other ways. For example, this eating system provides the right balance of carbohydrates to proteins to fats. That will help to normalize blood sugar and insulin levels. High insulin levels have been shown to increase hunger as well as to promote the storage of belly and hip and thigh fat! Also, the plate will help you to continue to eat the foods you love as well as a few crucial foods that will help turn down your appetite and turn up your fat-burning furnace. Finally, the plate will help you maximize your consumption of high-fiber foods, which are important for your bowel health. Many people neglect their bowel health when trying to firm their bodies. The fact of the matter is that if wastes fail to move smoothly through your bowels, they can leave you bloated—allowing your belly to bulge outward!

Here's how the Cruise Down Plate works. For breakfast, lunch, and dinner, place your food on a standard 9-inch dinner plate. Fill half the plate with vegetables (or fruit at breakfast) and the other half with equal portions of carbohydrate and protein foods, along with a teaspoon of fat. If you are still hungry, you can have another plate of vegetables. It's that easy!

Of course, I know there will be some of you out there with questions. You may wonder how high you can pile the food on your plate. Generally, no more than 1 to 1½ inches. To get a specific idea of the right protein, carbohydrate, and fat servings for your plate, spend a week measuring out your food portions, making a mental note as to how much space certain foods take up on your plate. After just 1 week, you'll be able to simply look at your plate—without measuring—and know you're on the right track.

After years of calorie counting, you may not feel confident using such a simple eating method, so on pages 29 to 33, I've included a few sample Cruise Down Plate meals and a food list to help you get started.

But whether you just eyeball your portions on your plate or use the sample meals, there's *no* starvation, *no* hunger, and *no* complicated arithmetic! By using my Cruise Down Plate eating system, you will never again have to count a **single calorie** or remember confusing details about portions and servings. Rather, the Cruise Down Plate will show you how to continue to eat the foods you love in the *right portions*.

I know it sounds too simple to be true. But as I've said, the plate will help you to eat the right balance of protein, fat, and carbohydrate. This is so important, particularly for creating lean muscle tissue. *Your muscles are made of protein and they repair and rebuild themselves with the protein from the food you eat!* In addition, eating some protein at every meal will help turn down hunger, as protein takes longer to digest than carbohydrate. And protein will also help keep your blood sugar levels stable.

Without an adequate carbohydrate supply, you cannot increase lean muscle. Yes, you heard right! You see, carbs are responsible for an insulin-mediated increase in the transport of amino acids from your bloodstream into your muscle tissue, which stimulates protein synthesis, prevents protein breakdown, and creates a positive nitrogen balance. Bottom line: *Don't* ever go "carb-free" if you want to avoid losing lean muscle.

Good fat on your plate is also critically important. Too often people who are trying to lose weight try to get their fat calories down to zero. They have heard that fat contains more calories per gram than carbohydrate or protein and that the body most efficiently shuttles fat into fat cells. However, this isn't completely accurate! Only some fats are bad for you. You need others to create a beautiful belly.

The bad ones? Saturated and hydrogenated fats found in animal products and fried and processed

body-bulging fats

Minimize these fats when trying to tone your body:

- Processed foods containing "partially hydrogenated fats"
- Margarine
- Shortening
- Fried foods

- Fatty cuts of beef and pork
- Chicken and turkey skins
- Butter
- Egg yolks

body-friendly fats

Eat more of these fats to help beautify your body:

- Flaxseed oil and ground flaxseeds (more on flax at www.jorgecruise.com)
- Extra-virgin olive oil and olives
- Avocados and guacamole
- Fatty cold-water fish such as salmon
- Nuts, especially almonds
- Almond butter
- Canola oil

foods. These are the fats that clog your arteries and lead to weight gain. They are found in fatty animal products (whole milk, cheese, fatty cuts of beef and pork) as well as fried and processed foods (fast foods, commercially baked goods, snack crackers and chips).

The good fats? Essential fatty acids found in flax seeds and flax products (such as flax meal, flax oil, and flax supplements), fish, nuts, avocados, olives, and olive oil. You need some dietary fat to boost your mood, aid muscle making, and make hormones. Fat also helps you feel satisfied, helping you to enjoy eating and stop before it's too late. A wealth of research is now finding that the key to weight loss is cutting back on saturated and hydrogenated fats and eating more essential fatty acids.

Finally, the vegetables on your Cruise Down Plate are packed with fiber, one of your most important body-beautifying secrets.

Fiber digests slowly, so it will help turn down your hunger. Fiber also helps keep insulin levels lower, preventing abdominal fat storage. Most important, fiber keeps your digestive tract running smoothly. Healthy digestion equals a beautiful belly! (In the bonus chapter on page 319, you will find tips for using fiber as well as other strategies to improve digestion and reduce bloating.)

In addition to following the Cruise Down Plate, I suggest you drink eight 8-ounce glasses of water a day. About 60 percent of your body is made up of water and your metabolism needs water in order to burn body fat for energy. Dehydration can slow fat burning. It also can sap your energy, making you too tired to do your Cruise Moves. Water also contains oxygen. In order for your lean muscle tissue to burn fat, it needs oxygen to help convert fat into energy. When you drink water, you improve your oxygen levels,

improving your metabolism.

You can meet your fluid requirements either with plain water—preferable because it has no calories—or with other non-caffeinated drinks and foods with high water contents, such as soup, fruits, and vegetables.

the three rules of the plate

Besides placing your foods on your plate in the right portions, you'll also follow three additional rules for optimal Cruise Down Plate success:

1. Eat breakfast within 1 hour of rising.
2. Eat every 3 hours.
3. Stop eating 3 hours before bed.

Here's why. To keep your metabolism running strong, you must eat your first meal within 1 hour of rising. As you sleep, your body is not getting any food and consequently turns down your metabolism. When you wake up, you want to kick your metabolism into high gear as soon as possible. If you don't eat within 1 hour of waking, your starvation protection system will kick in. And when that happens, your body will turn your metabolism down even more, making it really tough for you to burn off that lower body fat!

To keep your metabolism on the move, I also suggest you eat every 3 hours. This means you might eat breakfast at 7:00 A.M., then have a snack at 10:00 A.M., then eat lunch at 1:00 P.M., then a snack at 4:00 P.M., and finally dinner with a treat at 7:00 P.M.

These frequent mini meals will help prevent you from ever feeling over-hungry. When you allow yourself to get too hungry, you tend to overeat. Think back to times when you've eaten more food than you wished you had. Did you start your meal feeling ravenous?

Besides preventing overeating and food cravings, eating every 3 hours will also boost your metabolism! Yes, it's true. As your stomach and intestines grind up the food you eat and break it down into its simplest components, they burn up calories in the process. So spreading out

your food throughout the day helps you burn more calories through the process of digestion! Your snacks will also help to keep your blood sugar stable, again preventing sudden spikes in insulin that can lead to hunger and abdominal fat storage.

Finally, close the refrigerator and put an imaginary CLOSED sign in your kitchen 3 hours before you go to bed. When you eat 2 to 3 hours before going to sleep, you take too much food to bed with you, and your digestive system keeps you awake as it breaks down your food. Though you may actually be able to fall

A DAY OF EATING WITH THE CRUISE DOWN PLATE

Breakfast	Snack	Lunch	Snack	Dinner	Treat
Within 1 hour of rising	3 hours later	3 hours later (If you're still hungry, have another plate of veggies.)	3 hours later	3 hours later (If you're still hungry, have another plate of veggies.)	Eat before 7:30 PM (Or save for a mini-snack.)

To see more examples of breakfast, lunch, dinner, snacks, or treats go to pages 30–31.

asleep, you won't sleep deeply as your body digests. And you need *deep* sleep in order for your body to truly rest and recover from your Cruise Moves.

If you eat too late at night, your body spends its energy on digestion rather than on repairing and firming your lean muscle tissues. Your goal is to make sure that you recuperate during sleep rather than waste your rest on digestion. I promise you will feel more energized and alive when you wake!

the body cleanse

You'll notice in chapter 5 that I suggest you do a body cleanse each Saturday. Cleansing the body is so important, particularly to help create a firm and beautiful physique. Too often, toxins build up in our bodies from less-than-ideal eating habits. In particular, when you don't eat enough fiber throughout the week, it's hard for your body to efficiently move waste through your intestine. When intestinal waste gets stuck, gas builds up. This can result in bloating and abdominal distension—the last thing you want when trying to create a flat belly and leaner hips and thighs.

My Cruise Down Plate will help you to eat a healthful amount of fiber in order to keep your intestines running smoothly. However, one day a week (Saturday), I suggest you use this 3-step body cleanse.

Step 1. For breakfast, consume a shake made from psyllium seed husks. Psyllium is packed with fiber and has been shown in study after study not only to help keep you regular, but also to reduce cholesterol levels and to lower your hunger. Check out the online store at www.jorgecruise.com to purchase.

Step 2. Double your water intake. On your body cleanse day, you'll be increasing your fiber intake. You need to drink more water to mix with the fiber in your gut to help soften it to allow smooth passage. The extra water will also help to flush toxins out of your body. On Saturdays, drink eight 16-ounce glasses of water.

Step 3. Choose a non-meat source of protein for lunch and dinner. For example, you might have beans and rice, a bean burrito, or a hummus and vegetable sandwich. The fiber from the vegetable protein will also help clean out your pipes. You'll find examples of non-meat protein meals in the bonus chapter on page 319, along with other tips for creating your perfect body.

the dangers of emotional eating

Many people can easily follow the Cruise Down Plate and never feel tempted to overeat. But I know that some of you need a little extra help—particularly those of you who tend to eat for emotional, rather than physical, reasons.

What is emotional eating exactly? It's anytime you eat when you are not hungry and is the number one thing that can cause self-sabotage. How important is this? Well, I feel that what I am about to share with you is *the most important section of the book!* Indeed, if you don't master this step, you will never achieve a beautiful body.

In fact, you can do 8 minutes or 8 hours of abdominal exercises, but your belly will *never* shrink if you continue to overeat. A calorie is a calorie, and if you consume more calories than you burn, they will continue to go straight to those fat cells in your lower body and cover up the beautiful muscles that you want to show off!

Emotions rank as the number one most powerful cause of

overeating. Before they came to me for coaching, many of my clients used food as an emotional support for the distress in their lives. They lifted sadness with ice cream, covered up depression with chocolate chip cookies, and soothed anger with potato chips.

When I explored the cause of their emotional eating, I found that the true source of the problem stemmed from an emotional void or emptiness. They felt empty and they filled up that emptiness with food.

Think about it. In the past, when you ate when you were *not* hungry, did food help fill a void or numb a pain? Has food ever made you feel supported and comforted?

To stop the self-sabotage and end emotional eating, you must learn to discern between emotional hunger and nutritional hunger. Nutritional hunger is a biological need. It all about eating to provide your body with the building materials it needs to stay healthy and build lean muscle. Emotional hunger often comes from the lack of support, comfort, and warm nurturing from people. Only when you replace food with the support from friends and family will you be able to step off the emotional-eating roller coaster.

In my book, *8 Minutes in the Morning for Real Shapes, Real Sizes*, I created a powerful technique called *The People Solution*. It gave my clients strong protection from emotional eating. Since the publication of that book, I've heard tons of success stories from readers who tried it and loved it. The People Solution teaches you how to use the power of people to support you and replace the need and comfort of food. It includes three key tactics:

1. Become your own greatest friend. The first person in The People Solution is you. Too

renee hinton lost 3½ inches!

"I lost 2 inches in one thigh and 1½ inches in the other (my right thigh was larger than my left thigh to start with) and I have dropped 44 pounds!

"I loved these exercises because that is the area where I needed the most toning. It is a family genetic factor that I carry a lot of my weight in my thighs, and I was happy to shed those inches!!!

"I'm in my seventies now, and I am wearing the same size that I wore in my thirties. I love that I don't have to hide behind baggy clothes any more."

Renee lost 44 pounds!

often, people have a love-hate relationship with their bodies. Yet you must respect your body and treat it as the greatest gift you've ever received to experience success. Only when you respect your body will you firmly commit yourself to your Cruise Moves and feed your body healthful foods.

To help make that happen, I suggest all of my clients create what I call a "Power Pledge Poster." On the poster, they write the phrase, "My current body is the most precious gift I have ever been given." Underneath that, they write the positive consequences of believing that statement. For example, you might write, "I will treat my body as a top priority," or "I will feed my body properly." Then, underneath those consequences, write 10 sentences that describe why your body is a precious gift. For example, you might write, "My body helps me to get to where I need to go." I encourage you to create your own Power Pledge Poster. After you do so, photocopy it three times and post it in three spots in your house or at work where you will see it often.

2. Establish a support circle.
This is the second "people" of The People Solution. I encourage all of my clients to create a support network of—at minimum—three people that will help motivate them to stick to their program. Your inner circle can include family, coworkers, church members, and, of course, your good friends. You should choose people that allow you to feel comfortable communicating your feelings. Some of these people should be e-mail buddies—people you can e-mail at any time of the day or night when you feel you might be about to slip up. Others might be phone buddies—people who will agree to literally be on call in case you need support. One person should be an accountability buddy—someone you can meet with once a week to go over the specifics of the program along with your challenges and breakthroughs.

3. Expand your circle. In addition to picking three people you already know to help support your efforts, you will continually add more and more people to your inner circle. You might do that by joining or starting a "Jorge Cruise" weight-loss book group or by going online to JorgeCruise.com and meeting millions of Cruisers who are taking the same journey as you!

In *8 Minutes in the Morning for Real Shapes, Real Sizes*, I include many more specifics about The People Solution. However, you now know enough to get started. If you'd like more tips on incorporating The People Solution into your life, I suggest you pick up a copy of *8 Minutes in the Morning for Real Shapes, Real Sizes*.

more safety ahead

Since the publication of *8 Minutes in the Morning for Real Shapes, Real Sizes*, I found that, although The People Solution helped my clients to eliminate nearly all cases of emotional eating, some people still encountered *emergency emotional eating situations*, situations that I like to call Doughnut Moments.

To help my clients completely immunize themselves from even the most tempting of temptations, I created The Safety Belt System. It works like this. Think about driving down the road in a really safe car, such as a Volvo. You feel secure because you know the car was made specifically to protect you and the passengers in case of an accident. Were you to get in an accident, the Volvo's state-of-the-art frame would absorb the impact, keeping your body safe.

But even in a Volvo, you wouldn't drive down the road without your seatbelt, right?

That's the same principle here. My People Solution provides you with the safe car. It will help to reduce the emotional impact along the road to life. But you also want to be safe for sudden accidents that may toss you out of the car. You need a seatbelt to keep you safely behind the driver's seat of healthful eating and weight loss.

My Safety Belt System provides you with a set of strong seatbelts to help you overcome all situations that may drive you to eat emotionally. Just as race car drivers have multiple seatbelts to keep them extra safe on the road, you'll have multiple seatbelts to keep you *extra safe* in the kitchen, restaurants, cafeteria, or whenever you find yourself around food.

the safety belt system

With the help of millions of online and personal clients, I've come up with the following five "seatbelts" to help you prevent random acts of overeating.

Belt #1
The Audio Loop

This belt works a lot like self-hypnosis. For this seatbelt, you will create a digital or audiotape that you will listen to over and over again to help protect yourself from overeating. To make your tape, come up with very short answers to the following questions:

1. What will I lose in my life if I don't take care of myself?

For example, you might write, "If I fail to take good care of myself, I could lose my health, my energy, and my relationships."

2. What will I gain when I get healthy?

Here, you might write, "If I stick with the program, I'll be able to show off my belly, feel more confident, and live longer."

Keep your answers short. When you read them out loud, they should take less than 30 seconds to read. You will then record your answers into a tape or digital recorder. If you use a tape recorder, record onto a 1-minute self-looping tape (available at Radio Shack and other electronics stores). This will allow you to replay the message easily.

When you record your answers, play dramatic music softly in the background. I suggest you use scary background music such as the theme to *Jaws* for the first question and inspiring background music, such as the theme to *Chariots of Fire*, for the second question. Make two tapes—one for home and the other for travel.

You'll listen to your tape over and over again. It works a lot like a favorite song. Think of a song you've heard played over and over on the radio. After a while, you can hear it in your head without the song being on. That's the power of repetition and that's what this is all about.

The repetition will ingrain these concepts into your mind, helping to bolster your motivation to stick with your plan. For many years, scientists have known that such positive affirmations can help to dramatically improve health. As far back as the early 1900s a scientist named Emile Coué told his patients to say to themselves, "Every day in every way, I am getting better and better" 20 times every day. The affirmations were rumored to have improved their health! If such regular positive thoughts can improve your internal health, just imagine what they can do for your motivation to tone your body!

The Audio Loop has greatly helped Susan, one of my clients. Susan has a 20-minute commute home from work. She used to give in to cravings during her commute home and then feel guilty for nibbling on french fries and other types of fast food. Now she's overcome her fast food temptations with the Audio Loop. As soon as she gets into her car, she turns on her tape. "It really does get ingrained into the brain after only a few minutes," she told me. She listens to her affirmations all the way home. No matter how bad a day she had at work, she told me that she never stops for fast food on the way home.

Belt #2
Power Quotes

You can probably tell from reading this book that I love inspiring quotations. To me, there's nothing like reading the perfect quote at just the right moment to inspire me to eat right and stick to my fitness routines.

That's why I suggest you create a bunch of business cards with "power quotes" on them. That way, no matter where you find yourself, you can always whip out a business card and read a quote to help inspire you to success. To get started, search through quotation books or JorgeCruise.com

and jot down some quotes that you feel really help fuel your motivation. These don't just have to be quotes from famous people. You can jot down sayings that you see on bumper stickers, T-shirts, greeting cards, and even the casual motivational comments of friends or family members. Type your quotes into a word-processing program and print them out onto business cards. (You can purchase pre-perforated cards at an office supply store such as Staples, along with computer software that will help you easily print the quotes onto them.)

Once you've made your cards, laminate them and carry them with you. Look at them whenever you need a boost. For example, one of my clients carries a card with a quote from her husband. When she was struggling with an issue at work, he

remarked, "Temptation resisted is a true measure of character." The comment so struck her that she put it on a business card and carries it around with her, using it for a positive boost in any challenging situation.

Belt #3
Before and After Poster

One of my clients has placed a photo of herself at her highest weight ever on her fridge. Next to it, she has a photo of herself at her lowest weight ever. Whenever she feels tempted to raid the fridge, she sees the photos. "I think, 'Who do I want to be, the fat person on the left or the sexy and fit one on the right?' Unless I am physically hungry, I always choose the sexy and fit one and walk away from the fridge."

"I have my pictures on the pantry and the fridge—my two

Choose Your Belts

I want you to firmly commit yourself to using the Safety Belt System by writing down your three Seatbelts, and how you will use each one, in the space provided.

The three belts I will use are:

1. _____

2. _____

3. _____

Here is how I will incorporate each belt into my life:

1. _____

2. _____

3. _____

danger zones," says Reggie, another clients who uses the Before and After technique.

If you don't have an "after" photo of yourself, you can use a photo of a magazine model whom you'd like to emulate. Or you can cover your fridge with photos of beautiful bodies cut from magazines. Use whatever images will help you remember your goal.

Belt #4
Grab-and-Go Food Chart

You're most likely to eat unhealthy foods when you feel stressed or hurried. But you can avoid this problem with a little preparation. Take a moment to brainstorm a number of quick and healthy breakfasts, lunches, dinners, snacks, and treats. For example, you might keep a few frozen dinners on hand or grab a meal replacement shake along with an apple for a meal.

List as many grab-and-go meals as possible and then post your list on the fridge. This will also help make grocery shopping easier because you can consult your grab-and-go list to see what you need from the store.

Belt #5
The Home Run

This is so simple yet so powerful. I recommend that you set www.jorgecruise.com as your home page on your computer at work and at home. Whenever you go onto the Internet, my site will come up and you'll get a great reminder of your success. Every day on my site I post an inspiring quote that will help motivate you to stay on track. You can also ask me questions or go to any of the chat rooms or discussion boards for extra support. As one of my clients says, "When I am at work, I just turn my computer on and see Jorge's face and I feel like he is watching me and I wouldn't sabotage myself if you were physically here with me!"

the power of three

I've provided you with a variety of seatbelts. I want you to pick three that you feel will help keep you on track. Write them in the space provided on page 61. If you want to use more, that's great. But three is the minimum.

Your three belts will help you stick to your Cruise Down Plate, eating nutritionally rather than emotionally. Bottom line: If you eat nutritionally you will create lean muscle. If you eat emotionally you will create fat. The choice is yours.

My challenge to you right now is to choose to eat *nutritionally*. And to help you stop the emo-

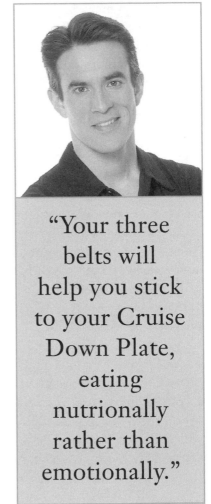

> "Your three belts will help you stick to your Cruise Down Plate, eating nutrionally rather than emotionally."

tional eating, use your top three safety belts, but also make sure to visit me at JorgeCruise.com, my online weight-loss club. There you will meet additional people to support you and help accelerate your weight loss. Before you know it, you will look and feel more beautiful and sexy than you ever have before.

sample meals for easy eating

If you're still not quite sure how to use the Cruise Down Plate, you'll find everything you need to know right here.

simple and delicious

For help on figuring out how to place foods on the plate in the correct portions, I've started you off with a few sample Cruise Down Plate meals. Just follow the photos on pages 30–31, and you'll get on track. Just remember: These are samples. To follow the Cruise Down Plate, you need only follow one simple rule: Fill half the plate with vegetables and the other half with equal portions of carbohydrate and protein foods, along with a teaspoon of fat. And if you are still hungry, have another plate of vegetables. It's that easy!

Use these photos for ideas and inspiration. Enjoy, and eventually you'll be creating your own delicious Cruise Down Plates in the right portions for weight loss. For even more sample meals and tips on using the Cruise Down Plate, please see *8 Minutes in the Morning for Real Shapes, Real Sizes.*

"Your goal for the Cruise Down Plate: Eat to support your lean muscle restoration."

one simple rule

Follow one simple rule for the Cruise Down Plate: Fill half your plate with vegetables, a quarter of your plate with carbohydrate foods, a quarter of your plate with protein foods, and use one teaspoon of fat.

Sample 1

Breakfast 1 cup milk with ½ cup Uncle Sam Cereal; ½ grapefruit; 6 almonds

Snack 3 celery sticks filled with 1 teaspoon peanut butter each

Lunch Sandwich (2 reduced-calorie slices of bread, 2 ounces turkey, 1 slice lean bacon, lettuce, sliced tomatoes); ⅛ avocado; 1 cup vegetable soup

Snack 30 raisins

Dinner Taco (2 ounces lean ground beef, 6-inch corn tortilla, 1 ounce fat-free shredded cheese, shredded lettuce, diced tomatoes, salsa); mixed green salad with 1 teaspoon flaxseed oil

Treat ½ tablespoon chocolate chips

Sample 2

Breakfast 6 scrambled egg whites; 1 small potato, cubed and sautéed in 1 teaspoon olive oil; 1 orange

Snack 1 string cheese stick

Lunch Taco salad (2 ounces ground turkey taco meat, 1 ounce fat-free shredded Cheddar cheese, 15 crumbled fat-free baked tortilla chips, 1 tablespoon oil-based salad dressing, shredded lettuce, diced tomato, onions, carrots)

Snack 1 cup air-popped popcorn sprinkled with Mrs. Dash seasoning

Dinner 3 ounces grilled salmon; ½ cup basmati rice; half-plate broccoli with 1 teaspoon flaxseed oil

Treat 1 Reese's Peanut Butter Cup

Sample 3

Breakfast 3 slices lean bacon; 2 4-inch pancakes with 1 cup sliced strawberries, 1 tablespoon reduced-calorie butter, and 2 tablespoons sugar-free syrup

Snack Low-fat granola bar

Lunch 1 sushi California roll (rice, crabmeat, cucumber, avocado, seaweed); 1 cup miso soup

Snack 1 piece peanut brittle

Dinner "Meat and potatoes" (3 ounces lean steak served with ½ cup roasted red potatoes); steamed carrots; mixed green salad with 1 teaspoon flaxseed oil

Treat Small fat-free cookie

Sample 4

Breakfast 1 cup low-fat yogurt mixed with ½ cup low-fat granola, 1 cup mixed berries, and 6 slivered almonds

Snack 2 cups baby carrots

Lunch Hot dog with 1 tablespoon mustard and ketchup on bun; mixed green salad with 1 teaspoon olive oil

Snack 20 peanuts

Dinner Sandwich (3 ounces grilled hamburger patty, sliced tomato and onion, 1 tablespoon ketchup, 1 tablespoon reduced-calorie mayo, served wrapped in iceberg lettuce); 10 to 15 french fries; 1 cup vegetable soup

Treat 1 cup frozen seedless grapes

cruise down plate optional food lists

As I shared with you in the beginning of this chapter, the Cruise Down Plate provides you the simplest method to support you in your goal of restoring your metabolism. There's no time-consuming calorie counting or banning of foods. As long as you fill the top half of your plate with veggies and the bottom half with equal portions of protein and carbohydrate foods along with 1 teaspoon of fat, you will provide your body the essential muscle-making materials to create new lean muscle—which will burn the fat!

some suggested guidelines

I've provided the following food lists to be used with your Jorge Cruise Planners on pages 61 and 197 as an optional resource for those of you who want a little more security during your first week or two with the Cruise Down Plate. If you ever feel confused about how much food to place on your Cruise Down Plate, consult my simple food lists on the following pages.

Use these lists to measure out your food portions for 1 week. After that, you should be able to automatically eyeball your food portions without the need of measuring cups and spoons. Think of your first week as your week of training. Soon, you'll be ready to take off your training wheels and ride effortlessly on the road to weight loss!

approximate caloric values

Although I have done all the counting for you, just for your reference here are the approximate caloric values of all the boxes found on the Jorge Cruise Planners on pages 61 and 197. All you need to do is check off the boxes on the planner and you are set!

Vegetable/Fruit	50
Fat	45
Carbohydrates	80
Protein	75
Snack	100
Treat	30–50

vegetables/ fruits

vegetables

Vegetables that are high in starch do not appear on this list; they are on the Carbohydrates list. For each specified vegetable amount, check off 1 Veggie box on your planner. All servings are 2 cups raw or 1 cup cooked, unless otherwise stated:

- Artichoke, medium
- Asparagus
- Beet greens
- Beets
- Bell peppers (green, yellow, red)
- Broccoli
- Brussels sprouts
- Carrots
- Cauliflower
- Chayote (squash)
- Collard greens
- Eggplant
- Green beans
- Kale
- Leeks
- Mung bean sprouts
- Onions
- Parsnips
- Pea pods
- Pickles (3 large)
- Rutabaga
- Sauerkraut

- Seaweed, raw
- Snow peas
- String beans
- Tomatillo, raw (2 medium)
- Tomato (2 medium)
- Tomato paste (6 tablespoons)
- Tomato puree (1 cup)
- Tomato sauce (1 cup)
- Tomatoes, canned (1 cup)
- Turnips
- Vegetable soup, fat-free, low sodium (1 cup)

fruit

For each specified amount, check off 1 Fruit box on your Jorge Cruise Planner. If you can't find a particular fruit listed, check off 1 box for every small to medium fresh fruit, ½ cup of canned fruit, or ¼ cup dried fruit. Ideally, eat fruit only for breakfast due to its higher simple sugar content.

- Apples, green or red (1 medium)
- Apple juice (½ cup)
- Applesauce, unsweetened (½ cup)
- Apricots (4)
- Bananas (½ medium)
- Blackberries (¾ cup)
- Blueberries (¾ cup)
- Cantaloupe (⅓ melon, or 1 cup cubed)
- Cherries (12 large)
- Cranberry juice (½ cup)
- Fruit cocktail (½ cup)

- Grapefruit (½)
- Grapefruit juice (½ cup)
- Grapes, green or red (12)
- Honeydew (⅛ melon, or 1 cup cubed)
- Kiwifruit (1 large)
- Orange (1 medium)
- Peach (1 medium)
- Pear, green (1 small)
- Pineapple, canned, packed in juice (⅓ cup)
- Plum (2 medium)
- Prunes (2)
- Raisins (2 tablespoons)
- Raspberries (1cup)
- Strawberries (1 cup)
- Watermelon (1 cup cubed)

fats

For each specified amount, cross off 1 Fat box on your Jorge Cruise Planner.

preferred fats

- Almond butter (1 tablespoon) PLUS 1 Protein box
- Almonds, raw (6)
- Avocado (⅛ medium)
- Cashews (6)
- Flax oil (1 teaspoon or 4 capsules)
- Oil-based salad dressing (1 tablespoon)
- Olive oil (1 teaspoon)
- Olives (10 small or 5 large)

- Peanut butter (2 teaspoons) PLUS 1 Protein box
- Peanuts (10)
- Pecans (4 halves)
- Pumpkin seeds (1 tablespoon)
- Sesame seeds (1 tablespoon)
- Soy mayonnaise (1 tablespoon)
- Sunflower seeds (1 tablespoon)
- Tahini paste (2 teaspoons)

fats to minimize

- Butter, reduced-calorie (1 tablespoon)
- Butter, stick (1 teaspoon)
- Butter, whipped (2 teaspoons)
- Coconut (2 tablespoons)
- Cream cheese (1 tablespoon)
- Cream cheese, reduced-calorie (2 tablespoons)
- Half-and-half (2 tablespoons)
- Mayonnaise (1 teaspoon)
- Mayonnaise, reduced-calorie (1 tablespoon)
- Shortening (1 teaspoon)
- Sour cream (2 tablespoons)
- Sour cream, reduced-calorie (3 tablespoons)

carbohydrates

For each specified amount, check off 1 Carbohydrate box on your Jorge Cruise Planner. Higher-fat selections will require you to check off 1 or 2 Fat boxes in addition to the complex Carbohydrate box. If you can't find a particular complex carbohydrate listed, check off one box for every ½ cup of cereal, grain, pasta, or starchy vegetable.

breads

- Bagel (½ of a 2-ounce bagel)
- Bread (1 ounce or 1 slice)
- English muffin (½)
- Hamburger roll (½)
- Nan (bread from India) (¼ of 8" x 2" loaf)
- Pita, 6-inch (1/2)
- Roll, dinner (1 small)
- Tortilla, corn, 6-inch (1)
- Tortilla, flour, 7-inch (1)
- Waffle, fat-free (1)

cereals and grains

- Barley, cooked (½ cup)
- Basmati rice (⅓ cup)
- Brown rice, cooked (⅓ cup)
- Buckwheat (Kasha), cooked (½ cup)
- Bulgur, cooked (½ cup)
- Cereal, cold, sweetened (½ cup)
- Cereal, cold, unsweetened (¾ cup)—Uncle Sam Cereal is Jorge's favorite!
- Cereal, hot (½ cup)
- Couscous, cooked (½ cup)
- Granola, low-fat (½ cup)
- Hominy grits, cooked (½ cup)

- Wheat germ (3 tablespoons)
- Wild rice, cooked (⅓ cup)

flour

- Cornstarch (2 tablespoons)
- Matzo meal (⅓ cup)
- Whole wheat flour, all purpose (2½ tablespoons)

pasta

- All varieties cooked such as spaghetti, linguine, noodles, penne (½ cup)

starchy vegetables

- Corn (½ cup)
- Corn on the cob (6-inch ear)
- French fries (10) PLUS 1 Fat box
- Green peas (½ cup)
- Potato, baked (1 small)
- Potato, instant (⅓ cup)
- Potato, mashed (½ cup)
- Pumpkin (½ cup)
- Sweet potato (⅓ cup)
- Winter squash, acorn or butternut (¾ cup)
- Yucca root (cassava), boiled (½ cup)

crackers

- Matzo (¾ ounce)
- Melba toast (4 slices)
- Oyster crackers (24)
- Saltine crackers (6)
- Whole wheat crackers (2–5)

protein

For each specified amount, check off 1 Protein box on your Jorge Cruise Planner. Higher-fat selections will require you to check off 1 or 2 Fat boxes in addition to the Protein box. Meat protein sources are based on cooked portions; raw meat will shrink when cooking. A 4-ounce raw chicken breast will shrink to 3 ounces when cooked.

beans

- Black, cooked (½)
- Chickpeas, cooked (½)
- Hummus (¼ cup) PLUS 1 Fat box
- Kidney, cooked (½)
- Lentil, cooked (½)
- Lima , cooked (½)
- Pinto, cooked (½)
- Refried, fat-added (⅓ cup) PLUS 1 Fat box
- Refried, fat-free (⅓ cup)
- Split peas, cooked (½ cup)
- White, cooked (½ cup)

cheese (55 calories or less per ounce)

- American (1 ounce)
- Cheddar (1 ounce)
- Cottage, low-fat or fat-free (¼ cup)
- Feta (1 ounce)
- Monterey Jack (1 ounce)
- Muenster (1 ounce)
- Parmesan, grated (1 tablespoon)
- Provolone (1 ounce)
- Ricotta, low-fat or fat-free (¼ cup)
- Soy, all varieties (1 ounce)
- Swiss (1 ounce)

milk products

- Lactose-free milk, low-fat or fat-free (8 ounces)
- Milk, 1% or fat-free (8 ounces)
- Milk, whole (8 ounces) PLUS check off 2 Fat boxes
- Nonfat dry milk (⅓ cup)
- Soy milk, fortified, 1% or fat-free (8 ounces)
- Yogurt, frozen, low-fat or nonfat (½ cup)
- Yogurt, low-fat or nonfat, flavored (8 ounces) PLUS check off 2 Fruit boxes
- Yogurt, low-fat or nonfat, plain (8 ounces)
- Yogurt, whole milk, plain (8 ounces) PLUS check off 2 Fat boxes

eggs

- Egg, whole (1)
- Egg substitute (¼ cup)
- Egg whites (3)

poultry

- Chicken or turkey, white meat without skin (1 ounce)
- Chicken or turkey, dark meat with skin (1 ounce) PLUS 1 Fat box

fish, canned

- Salmon, packed in water (¼ cup)
- Sardines, packed in water (2 medium)
- White tuna, packed in water (¼ cup)

fish, fresh or frozen

- Fried fish (1 ounce) PLUS 1 Fat box
- Mahi Mahi (1 ounce)
- Salmon (1 ounce)
- Sea bass (1 ounce)
- Sole (1 ounce)
- Swordfish (1 ounce)
- Tuna (1 ounce)

shellfish

- Clams (2 ounces)
- Crab (2 ounces)
- Crawfish (2 ounces)
- Lobster (2 ounces)
- Oysters (6 medium)
- Scallops (2 ounces)
- Shrimp (2 ounces)

soy products

- Soybeans , cooked (½)
- Soy burger (½ burger)
- Soy cheese (1 ounce)
- Soy hot dog (1)

- Soy milk, fortified, 1% or fat-free (8 ounces)
- Texturized soy protein (1 teaspoon or 1 ounce)
- Tofu (½ cup)

red meats

- Bacon (1 slice) PLUS 1 Fat box
- Goat (1 ounce)
- Ham, smoked or fresh (1 ounce)
- Hot dog, beef, pork, or combination (1) PLUS 2 Fat boxes
- Lamb shank or shoulder (1 ounce)
- London broil (1 ounce)
- Round steak (1 ounce)
- Sirloin steak (1 ounce)
- Skirt steak (1 ounce)
- Tenderloin (1 ounce)
- Veal chop or roast (1 ounce)

snacks

For each specified amount, check off 1 snack box on your Jorge Cruise Planner. In general, your snacks are about 100 calories.

- Almonds (12)
- Angel food cake (2-ounce slice)
- Baby carrots (2 cups)
- Baker's cookie (www.bbcookies.com) (1)
- Brownie (1)
- Butterscotch (4 pieces)
- Candy corn (20 pieces)
- Cashews (12)

- Celery (3 sticks with 1 teaspoon of peanut butter on each)
- Chocolate-covered almonds (7)
- Fruit, 1 piece (see fruit lists for portion size)
- Fudge (1 ounce)
- Gelatin (½ cup)
- GeniSoy Soy Crisps (25)
- Granola bar, low-fat (1)
- Gumdrops (1 ounce)
- Heath bar (1 snack size)
- Hershey's milk chocolate bar (1 small)
- Hershey's milk chocolate bar with almonds (1 small)
- Hershey's Sweet Escapes (1 bar, any kind)
- Kit Kat (1 2-piece bar)
- Kudos with M&M's granola bar (1)
- Melba toast (4 slices)
- No Pudge! Fat Free Fudge Brownie (www.nopudge.com) (1 2" square)
- Oyster crackers (24)
- Peanut brittle (1 ounce)
- Peanuts (20)
- Pecans (8 halves)
- Popcorn, air popped (3 cups)
- Potato chips, fat-free (15–20)
- Pound cake (1-ounce slice)
- Pretzels (¾ ounce)
- Pudding cup, fat-free (1)
- Pumpkin seeds (2 tablespoons)
- Raisins (30)
- Rice cakes (2)

- Saltine crackers (6)
- Sesame seeds (2 tablespoons)
- Sherbet (½ cup)
- Skinny Cow fat-free fudge bar (1)
- Skinny Cow low-fat ice cream sandwich (½)
- String cheese (1)
- Sunflower seeds (2 tablespoons)
- Tofutti (¼ cup)
- Tortilla chips, fat-free (15–20)
- Uncle Sam Cereal (½ cup dry)
- Whole wheat crackers (2–5)
- Whoppers malted milk balls (9)
- Yogurt, frozen, low-fat or nonfat (½ cup)
- Yogurt, low-fat or nonfat (8 ounces)

treats

For each specified amount, check off 1 treat box on your Jorge Cruise Planner. Eat a delicious treat every day. In general, they should be 30 to 50 calories.

- Cheese slice, reduced-calorie (1)
- Chocolate chips (½ tablespoon)
- Chocolate-coated mints (4)
- Cookie, fat-free (1 small)
- Cranberry sauce (¼ cup)
- Frozen seedless grapes (1 cup)
- Gelatin dessert, sugar-free (1)
- Gingersnaps (3)
- Graham crackers (1 2½" square)
- Gumdrops (8 small)

- Hard candy (1)
- Hershey's Hugs or Kisses (2)
- Hershey's Miniatures (1, any kind)
- Jelly beans (7)
- Licorice twist (1)
- Oreo cookie (1)
- Marshmallow (1 large)
- M&M's (¼ of small bag)
- M&M's Minis (¼ of tube)
- Miss Meringue cookie (www.missmeringue.com) (1)
- Nonfat ice cream (½ cup) drizzled with Hershey's chocolate syrup
- Popcorn, air popped (1 cup)
- Reese's Peanut Butter Cup (1)
- SnackWell's sandwich cookie (1)
- York peppermint pattie (1 small)

alcohol

For maximum weight loss, alcohol should be kept to a minimum and limited to special occasions. Check off 1 snack box on your Jorge Cruise Planner for each of the specified amounts.

- Beer (12 ounces)
- Beer, light (12 ounces)
- Liquor (1½ ounces)
- Wine (5 ounces)

freebies

The following items do not need to be counted and you can con-
sume them as often as you like. These are great items to use if you want a second plate of food or more than your two daily snacks. Enjoy them!

vegetables

- Alfalfa sprouts
- Cabbage
- Celery
- Cucumber
- Garlic
- Green onions
- Jalapeño and other hot peppers
- Jicama
- Lettuce, all types (iceberg, loose leaf, romaine, spinach, watercress)
- Mushrooms
- Onions
- Radishes
- Zucchini

drinks

- Canarino Italian hot lemon drink (www.canarino.com)
- Carbonated or mineral water (add lime or lemon for great taste!)
- Coffee, plain
- Soft drinks, calorie-free
- Tea

Note: For each beverage you drink that contains caffeine you must increase your water intake by 2 extra glasses to stay hydrated.

seasonings

- Garlic
- Herbs, fresh or dried
- Kernel Season's Gourmet Popcorn Seasoning (www.kernelseasons.com— also excellent on pasta, vegetables, chicken, potatoes, eggs, and pitas!)
- Mrs. Dash
- Nonstick olive oil cooking spray
- Pimento
- Salsas, Tabasco, or hot pepper sauce
- Spices

condiments

- Horseradish
- Lemon juice
- Lime juice
- Mustard
- Soy sauce, light
- Vinegar
- Walden Farms salad dressings (www.waldenfarms.com)

sugar substitutes

- Equal
- Splenda (www.splenda.com)
- Sweet and Low
- SweetLeaf stevia products (www.steviaplus.com)—Jorge's favorite!

miscellaneous

- Sugar-free chewing gum
- Sugar-free gelatin

Part 2

Flat Belly Program

Introduction

I love this program. So far, *I have lost 40 pounds and 16 inches off my waist.* I have not felt this great in years. My doctor is blown away every time go in for a checkup. I am no longer on blood pressure medication, I have fewer headaches, and my knees don't ache like they used to before I lost weight. And when I look at pictures of me at my heaviest, I am astonished at just how big I really was! I knew I was heavy, but I never realized *how* big I was. I saved some of my "fat girl" clothes and now they are huge on me. That by itself is a big reward. I have not looked this good or felt this good in such a long time. It's like I finally found the right off-ramp that led me off the freeway of unhappiness. So many things change for the better in a person's life when they lose weight and live a healthy lifestyle.

Ann lost 16 inches!

It's amazing what a difference losing a few pounds can have on your life. Jorge's program is the answer. You do not need to spend endless hours in the gym, and you don't have to buy any costly exercise equipment. Since I started his program, I feel energized, I feel healthier, and I am much happier. I notice that I hold my body with better posture and that my muscles are becoming increasingly firmer. I would recommend Jorge's program to anyone. Some of my friends and family members have also been influenced by Jorge's program and I am excited to spread the news. **If anyone is out there wondering if this is the program for them, I wholeheartedly want YOU to know that *Jorge has the answers.*** If you are ready to make the commitment to take charge of your life, this is the answer. You can do it. Jorge's program is simple, rewarding, and livable. It will change your life for the better. Let this be the day you make the commitment to change. You can do it. I know you can.

—Ann Kirkendall, JorgeCruise.com client

abdominal fat's dirty little secret

Before you embark on my exciting *8 Minutes in the Morning for a Perfect Body* program, let's first take a look at why you want to create a beautiful belly. Many people want to tone their bellies for visual reasons. Not a day goes by that one of my clients doesn't ask me how she can look better in a swimsuit. Some tell me that they desperately want to zip up a particular pair of jeans. Or they just want to be able to look down and not see a bulge!

Those are all good reasons. But there are a few crucial and even more important reasons to start my *8 Minutes in the Morning for a Perfect Body* program.

Here's the real bad news about abdominal fat. Belly fat is worse for your health than fat in your butt or thighs. Yes, belly fat tends to trigger your liver to release its stored fatty acids—raising your cholesterol levels. It also tends to alter levels of key hormones involved in appetite, fat storage, and heart disease. In fact, when you gain weight in your abdomen, and these hormones become altered, you tend to feel hungrier, you eat more, and your body tends to store more fat in your abdomen. It's a vicious cycle—but you *can* break it!

Before we talk about how you will break your belly fat cycle, let's first take a look at all of the ways it erodes your health.

Diabetes. Research shows that women with a waist circumference of 36 inches or more are five times more likely to develop diabetes than those with smaller waist circumferences. When you gain weight in your abdomen, the fat throws off your insulin cycle. This important hormone, produced by the pancreas, is supposed to shuttle blood sugar into muscle cells so that those cells can burn it for energy. However, in people who have a lot of abdominal fat, insulin stops working properly. The muscle cells fail to respond to insulin and sugar remains high in the blood. This makes the pancreas release more and more insulin, which can eventually wear out your pancreas and develop into diabetes. At the same time, high levels of insulin trigger you to eat by making you feel hungry. They also encourage your liver to convert your blood sugar into fat—for storage! High insulin levels have also been linked with certain cancers.

Heart disease. In Harvard's famed Nurse's Health Study of 4,470 women, those with a waist circumference of 32 inches or more were twice as likely to

suffer a heart attack as those with smaller waists. Just as belly fat causes diabetes, it also raises blood cholesterol levels, contributing to heart disease. As your liver converts more and more blood sugar into fat, your cholesterol levels go up as this fat must make its way through your blood stream and into

"Women with a waist circumference of 36 inches or more are five times more likely to develop diabetes."

waiting fat cells—usually in your belly! In particular, the unhealthy LDL cholesterol and triglyceride levels rise, whereas the healthy HDL cholesterol takes a nosedive. Belly fat raises your risk for high blood cholesterol by 50 percent.

Breast cancer. The more body fat you have—particularly in your abdomen—the higher your estrogen levels. Body fat produces its own estrogen, in addition to the estrogen produced by your ovaries. Usually, this doesn't cause problems. But when you have a large amount of body fat, you risk raising estrogen levels too high, increasing your risk for breast cancer. Also, as I've already mentioned, belly fat tends to raise insulin levels—which also have been linked with breast cancer. Women with high levels of belly fat are 45 percent more likely to have breast cancer. Belly fat also raises your risk for endometrial cancer.

High blood pressure. Excess belly fat raises your risk for high blood pressure by 60 percent. In fact, each pound of extra fat can raise your systolic (top) blood pressure number by 4.5 points. It does so because your heart must work harder to pump blood to a larger body. It's the same as if you added many rooms onto an existing house but kept the same furnace. The furnace would have to work overtime to heat the larger house. In this case, your heart beats faster and more forcefully. This forces blood with more pressure through your arteries, causing nicks and dents to the linings of your arteries, raising your risk for heart disease.

Back pain. Fat in your belly acts like a heavy weight that pulls your lower spine forward, overly arching your lower back and causing pain. When you lose the fat and strengthen your abdomen, your belly muscles can better support your spine, improving your posture and reducing back pain.

Fatigue. Just as your heart can't grow larger to respond to the demands of a larger body, the same goes for your lungs. They now must work harder to supply more oxygen. Also, as your belly grows larger, it crowds out your internal organs, particularly the diaphragm muscle that's so important in breathing. People with a lot of belly fat tend to cough and wheeze more. Belly fat also raises your risk for sleep apnea, a severe form of snoring in which your windpipe repeatedly collapses throughout the night, causing your body to starve for oxygen.

Varicose veins. Excess body weight makes it harder for the blood in your legs to travel against the force of gravity back up to your heart. Belly fat also weighs down the veins in your upper thighs. Both problems cause the veins to weaken. Eventually they begin to leak and even allow blood to pool and travel backward, causing varicose veins.

Joint pain. The heavier your body, the more it weighs down your joints and the more impact you inflict on your joints with every step.

In addition, belly fat has also been linked to chronic pain, gallbladder disease, arthritis, low immunity, liver disease, skin problems, and poor sleep. It's time to put an end to this vicious health-eroding cycle once and for all!

the benefits of a firm belly

Losing weight in your midsection will help you prevent all of those diseases and conditions. You'll live longer and feel better!

My special Cruise Moves (you'll learn more about them in chapter 4) will do even more. They will help strengthen

Beautiful Belly Basics

Here are some of the most common questions and comments I've received from my online clients about their bellies.

I've been doing 100 crunches every day for the past month and my belly is still as big as ever. What gives?

You may not be doing the most effective exercises for your belly. You need to target and isolate **four important belly areas** in order to create a firm belly. That means you must do four *different* exercises. You can experience faster, better results by doing fewer repetitions of four different exercises than you can by spending more time with just one exercise. That's why each of my belly routines includes four *different* Cruise Moves.

I'm convinced that my metabolism is shot. Will anything help me lose weight?

Your metabolism may indeed be slower than normal, particularly if you've dieted over and over again. (You'll find out why dieting is bad in chapter 4.) But you can give your metabolism a swift kick by building lean muscle. Each pound of lean muscle burns 50 calories a day—just to maintain itself. (You should have read about this in chapter 3.)

I started a running program but my belly is still big. What's going on?

Running is actually counterproductive to creating a beautiful belly. Running burns up lots of calories, but it tends to pull your pelvis forward, overly arching your lower back. Take a look at a few runners—particularly the ones who don't do any form of abdominal strengthening. Chances are that they have belly bulges, too! When the lower spine overly arches, the pelvis tips forward and the belly pooches outward. You don't have to give up running—especially if you love doing it—but you need to combine it with my Cruise Moves program to see true results.

I've lost all the weight I want, but my lower belly still seems to bulge outward. What can I do?

That's where my program comes in. Weight loss alone won't tone and beautify those belly muscles. You need specific exercises that target the right belly areas. My Cruise Moves will do just that!

Are abdominal crunches the most important belly exercise?

No. The traditional crunch allows you to cheat in a multitude of ways. Plus it works only one part of your abdomen. I've found that most people absolutely *hate* doing crunches. If you hate doing it and it doesn't work that effectively, I say, don't do them. **None of my Cruise Moves involve abdominal crunches.**

My belly will never be toned, so why bother?

That's not true. I've had clients who thought the same thing and they look great now! Believe in yourself and stick with the program and you will soon be showing off that beautiful belly!

I don't want my belly to look muscular, like a man's. What can I do?

Women don't have the hormones to build huge, bulky muscles. If you're a woman, my Cruise Moves will give you the soft, toned look you seek.

the muscles in your abdomen, providing a number of exciting benefits.

Most important, stronger abdominal muscles help to automatically improve your posture. Strong abdominal muscles help support your spine, helping to keep it erect and long. They also help to hold your pelvis in the correct position, preventing the swayback so often seen after pregnancy and with increasing age. Once you eliminate that swayback, the rest of the spine tends to fall into line, allowing you to bring back your shoulders and head and stand taller and more upright.

In fact, even if you don't lose any weight, your appearance will improve dramatically. Stronger abdominal muscles will help you stand taller, creating a leaner appearance. You will feel as if you have grown an inch taller and slimmed an inch in the process—just by improving your posture!

Better posture, in turn, helps you breathe more deeply. Your abdominal muscles help you to inhale and exhale, allowing you to take fuller, deeper breaths.

Your abdominal muscles were designed for endurance. They were made to work 24 hours a day without getting fatigued. The rest of the muscles in your body were not designed this way. When your abdominal muscles support your spine, other muscles don't have to work overtime to keep you upright. You will find that as you strengthen your abdominal muscles and improve your posture, headaches and neck and shoulder pain will subside.

Your abdominal muscles are your power center. The stronger they are, the stronger you are. You will find that, by strengthening your abs, you have the energy to do more. If you play sports, your movements will be more powerful. You'll be able to sit at work for a longer period of time without feeling fatigued. Strong abdominal muscles help you to more easily lift, bend, twist, balance, and coordinate all of your movements.

Indeed, your abdominal muscles help you do just about everything!

why 8 Minutes in the Morning for a Perfect Body is your answer

You will love *8 Minutes in the Morning for a Perfect Body*! If you follow the program, you can expect to see noticeable results within 4 weeks.

8 Minutes in the Morning for a Perfect Body makes your goal simple and easy. And that's important. You may be able to beautify your belly by exercising for 60 minutes or more a day. But are you going to keep that up? To keep your belly toned, you must keep up the effort. You can do so only if your program is simple, efficient, and practical. That's what the Jorge Cruise® programs are all about! You'll be able to create a beautiful belly and keep it that way because you are finally embarking on a sustainable program. It's that simple!

Are you motivated to start toning and firming your belly? *Get ready to stop doing aerobics and step off the dieting roller coaster.* My challenge to you right now is that you commit to creating beautiful lean muscle. By doing so, you will reshape your body and sculpt a gorgeous and beautiful belly in just 8 minutes a day. **Your friends will compliment you on your appearance and you'll be able to wear swimsuits and belly shirts with confidence.** So get ready to feel that new confidence soar and turn the page to find out more about my groundbreaking *8 Minutes in the Morning for a Perfect Body* program.

Chapter 4
8 Minute Moves

the contractor and the work

I told you in the previous chapter about how creating a firm belly is a lot like building a house. I told you that when you build your house, your first step involves hiring your contractor—the person who does the physical work. Now you are ready to hire the contractor for your body, the person who will do the physical work needed to build a toned belly.

"My program requires only 8 minutes a day to achieve the same amount of lean muscle creation as other programs."

That contractor is you! Yes, you will initiate the transformational "8 minute" work needed to build the beautiful belly that you seek. In this chapter, you will learn every-thing you need to know about the physical work—Cruise Moves—needed to achieve your goal. In chapter 3, you have already learned all about the building materials—the eating plan—you will use to achieve success.

Here's the really exciting news about Cruise Moves. They make the physical work needed to build a beautiful belly a lot easier than the work needed to build a house! My unique resistance-training moves take only 8 minutes a day. I challenge you to commit to taking the first step of the Jorge Cruise® weight-loss revolution. By doing so, you will discover the most efficient, simple, and easy way to shed fat and tone your belly.

your "8 minute" edge

Cruise Moves make your journey to a flat belly simple and easy. Cruise Moves allow you to:

• Exercise for only 8 minutes a day

• Exercise in the comfort of your own home

• Create the muscle needed to burn the fat

• Feel more vibrant and confident

how focused cruise moves work

Now, more about Cruise Moves, your most important metabolism-boosting weapon.

Cruise Moves are unique resistance-training exercises that take just 8 minutes a day to complete. They involve minimal equipment and *absolutely no stomach crunches!* You can roll out of bed and do them in your favorite pair of pajamas in the privacy of your own home.

Other resistance-training programs require you to exercise most of the major muscle groups of your body in one very long session, working out every other day to allow the muscles to recover. To me, this is not only a waste of valuable time, but also not the most effective way to burn fat. These programs require you to spend an hour or more at a gym each day, whereas my program requires only 8 minutes a day to achieve the same amount of muscle creation.

Yet, while Cruise Moves may create the same amount of muscle as those other programs, they will actually help you burn many more calories. You see, your body burns calories at a higher rate for 12 to 24 hours *after* a resistance-training session. I like to call this the *afterburn* because your metabolic rate skyrockets as your body goes to work repairing and strengthening your muscles.

My Cruise Moves will enable your body to create that lean, fat-burning muscle that I just mentioned. On pages 64 to 175, you will find three levels ranging from very gentle to very challenging.

Start with Level 1. Stick with Level 1 for 4 weeks before moving onto Level 2. Then do that program for 4 weeks before moving onto Level 3. Four weeks will give your body the time it needs to adapt to the Cruise Moves. Within 4 weeks, you will have created enough muscle to allow you to tackle the next level with ease. (*Note:* Level 1 may feel too easy for you right away. If you don't feel challenged by the exercises, move up to Level 2 after just 1 week with Level 1.)

For every level of the program, you will follow the same schedule. Three days a week—on Mondays, Wednesdays, and Fridays—you will focus on Cruise Moves that zero in on your main trouble spot—your abdomen. On Tuesdays, you will do Cruise Moves that target your upper body (chest, shoulders, and arms). On Thursdays, you'll do Cruise Moves for your lower body (lower back and legs). Consult "Your Cruise Moves Schedule" on page 50.

No matter whether you are targeting your abdomen, your upper body, or your lower body, you will tackle your Cruise Moves session in the same manner. *Each session includes four different moves.* You will perform each move for 1 minute and then proceed directly on to the next move. I've strategically paired the moves so that you never need to rest between them. Once you've completed all four moves, you'll repeat them all one more time for 1 minute each—for a total of 8 minutes.

You either hold or pump through the suggested Cruise Move for up to 1 minute, and then move on to the next Cruise Move. This frees your mind from counting and forces you to fully fatigue the muscle you are working. It's simple. It's convenient. You'll love it.

I've found with much trial and error in testing this program on my clients that 60 seconds is the optimal amount of time needed to start firming your muscles. In testing this program on client after client, I have found it ideal.

your cruise moves for the belly

Let's take a closer look at your Cruise Moves for Mondays, Wednesdays, and Fridays. These are the days that you will specifically target your trouble zone—your belly.

Too often, people try to flatten their bellies the wrong way. They do just one exercise—often an abdominal crunch—over and over and over again. This is not an efficient way to tone your belly!

First, abdominal crunches work only one area of your abdomen—the part along the front of your belly above the belly button. Unfortunately, this happens to be the one area of the belly that's often strongest for most people! So crunches simply make an already strong area of the abdomen even stronger, ignoring important weak spots that are the true source of your problem.

Second, I've never met anyone who enjoys doing abdominal crunches. My clients have complained to me over and over

about how crunches feel awkward and make their *necks hurt*. I don't believe in forcing yourself to do an exercise that you don't like. That's why none of my Cruise Moves include crunches!

As I've said, to truly create a slender waist and flat belly, you must strengthen your entire abdomen. That means doing moves that address the following areas:

The upper rectus abdominus. This large muscle forms the much-sought-after "six-pack" along the front of your abdomen. Though it appears to be made up of four to six smaller muscles, it's really one large muscle broken up with striations of connective tissue. The rectus abdominus (upper and lower) starts at your sternum in your chest and runs all the way down to your pubic bone. The upper portion of this muscle ends at your navel. As I've said, this is often the strongest muscle in the abdomen.

The lower rectus abdominus. Even though your rectus abdominus is actually one sheet of muscle, not two, we trainers often refer to the lower and upper areas as separate units because you must do different exercises to address them. Your lower area is on the front of your belly below the navel. This area

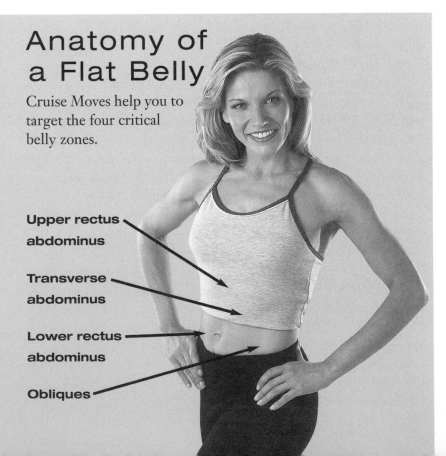

Anatomy of a Flat Belly

Cruise Moves help you to target the four critical belly zones.

Upper rectus abdominus

Transverse abdominus

Lower rectus abdominus

Obliques

is often particularly weak in women after childbirth.

The obliques. Your obliques are located along the sides of your abdomen. They start at the tip of your hipbones and end at your rib cage. They help you to twist or bend your body from side to side. Strengthening them helps to shrink love handles and slim your waist. Strong obliques are the key to cinching your belt one notch tighter.

The transverse abdominus. This corsetlike muscle wraps around your pelvis, just below your rib cage. It's the muscle you use when you suck in your gut or cough or sneeze. It's also the most neglected of abdominal muscles, primarily because so few traditional moves work this area. Your transverse abdominus is very important because it helps to hold your internal organs in place. It also helps support your lower back and stabilize your torso during certain movements, such as heavy lifting. A strong transverse abdominus gives you balance and coordination in all of your daily movements. This is why in fitness classes you're told to suck in your belly. That makes you flex your transverse abdominus to support your spine.

Few of us use our transverse muscle very much. Because it acts to stabilize your torso, it only

works when you are moving. But most of us sit all day long, allowing this muscle to become woefully weak. When it weakens, it doesn't do a good job of holding in your internal organs in place, allowing your abdomen to bulge.

the core four

Every Monday, Wednesday, and Friday you will address all four belly areas with what I like to call my *Core Four*. You'll notice that my Cruise Moves are a bit different than the typical abdominal exercises you may have seen. In many of my Cruise Moves you will use your body weight to add a stability challenge to your midsection, working not just your abdomen but also your entire core—your back, butt, sides, *and* abdomen. This is the key to standing taller, stronger, and slimmer. My Cruise Moves will not only help strengthen and beautify your belly, but also help you to function more easily in everyday life.

Here are some tips to help you make the most of your Cruise Moves.

Exhale as you contract your abs. Exhaling when you contract any muscle—for example, during the *up* phase of a push-up or as you *raise* your arms during a biceps curl—will help you unleash

an extra bit of internal strength to perform the movement. Exhaling during the contraction is particularly important for abdominal moves.

Exhaling—even somewhat forcefully—will help in two ways. First, it will help you to better activate your transverse abdominus muscle. Second, if you inhale on the contraction, you risk outwardly shaping your belly muscles. You may still develop strong muscles, but you'll have strong muscles shaped in the wrong position.

Go slowly and deliberately. Don't rush through your Cruise Moves. Slow down and focus your attention on quality and *not* on quantity. Research shows that you will recruit more muscle fibers the more slowly you move. This will make your sessions more efficient. Second, moving more slowly will help you to concentrate on using proper form and making the most of each movement.

Maintain a neutral spine. In many of my moves I will suggest that you keep your spine long and straight. This will help protect your lower back and neck. I've noticed that many people *think* their spine is in the proper position, even when it's not. To find out what a neutral spine feels like, stand with your back and shoulders against the wall. Because of the natural S-curve in your spine, your lower back and neck won't be completely against the wall. However, everything else—including your ribs, shoulders, and head—should be against the wall. This is proper spinal alignment. Try to use it in most of your moves.

your equipment

If you've read any of my other books, then you know that I try to incorporate as little equipment as possible into my routines. I want you to be able to do your routines wherever you find yourself—at home, at a hotel room, at a friend's house. That way you have no excuses to skip your session!

The vast majority of my Cruise Moves include absolutely no equipment, other than chairs and other furniture common in most houses and hotel rooms. However, for some routines, I've included a few crucial yet inexpensive items. You can find your equipment at any sporting goods store for a very minimal investment, usually less than $20. And you can easily store it behind a couch or in a closet.

You will need:

• **A heavy ball.** These weighted balls (also called medicine balls)

will help add resistance to your routines. Start with a weight of 5 pounds.

• **A large fitness ball.** These plastic, air-filled balls (also called Swiss balls) will add a balancing challenge to your routine, making you recruit more muscles to complete the same movements.

the power of the morning

Many people ask me, "Now Jorge, why do you recommend doing the Cruise Moves in the morning? I don't understand. I'm not a morning person, I like working out in the afternoon or in evening."

Well, I truly believe that there's no such thing as not being a morning person. I know this in part because I used to be a victim of the same belief.

I used to stay up late at night because I told myself that I was a *night person*. I would read, watch TV, and talk on the phone into the morning's wee hours. It's no wonder I always felt tired when my alarm went off in the morning. I never got enough sleep!

When I first tried to exercise in the morning, I thought the task was an impossibility. "Maybe morning exercise works for some people," I told myself, "but it certainly doesn't work for me."

But a funny thing happened along the way. Each time I managed to actually get out of bed and exercise in the morning, I noticed that I felt wonderful for the rest of the day. As time wore on, I was able to get up earlier and earlier. I also felt sleepy earlier in the evening and naturally began going to bed earlier. I stopped being a night owl without really thinking about it.

These days, I never stay up later than 10 P.M., and I'm always out of bed by 6 A.M.

Now let me share with you three simple points that are going to motivate you to get up a bit earlier to do your moves. Once you understand the power of exercising in the morning, and of doing strength training in the morning, you're never going to go back to afternoon or evening workouts.

your cruise moves schedule

Each week you will work the following muscle groups in this order:

monday: belly
tuesday: upper body
wednesday: belly
thursday: lower body
friday: belly
saturday: body cleanse
sunday: day off

First, and most important for your belly, when you move in the morning, you're more likely to feel good for the rest of the day. You feel stronger, more energized, and less stressed. Remember, as I mentioned earlier, stress contributes to belly fat. When you move in the morning, you'll more likely handle deadlines and other hassles *without* setting off your fight-or-flight response.

Research backs this up. In a study at the University of Leeds in England, researchers found that women who exercised in the morning reported less tension and greater feelings of contentment for the rest of the day than those who didn't exercise in the morning. When you do your Cruise Moves, you send a signal to your pituitary gland to release endorphins, your body's natural feel-good chemicals. The more endorphins you have in your bloodstream, the better you feel. Thanks to morning exercise, you will be able to better handle stress no matter what happens in your day, whether it's getting stuck in a traffic jam, dealing with annoying coworkers, or tending to a sick child.

But that's not all. Moving in the morning also helps you to shed fat faster than moving at other times of the day. When you first wake up, your metabo-lism is sluggish because it has slowed down during sleep. But when you exercise, your metabo-lism increases. By doing your Cruise Moves first thing in the morning, you boost your metab-olism when it's normally the slowest. In short, you burn more calories when you exercise in the morning, making better use of your exercise time.

Finally, moving in the morning helps you to stay consistent. Have you ever *planned* to exercise in the afternoon or evening only to skip those plans because something else came up? That usually doesn't happen first thing in the morning. Simply put, the morning is your time. It's the eas-iest time to control. You can roll out of bed before your spouse or kids wake up, do your moves, and have some extra time just for you. Many of my clients say that their morning Cruise Moves provide a sort of moving meditation. It's the only time of the day that they have set aside just for them.

Remember, later in the day, distractions will come up. Your spouse, your children, your job, or an emergency will interrupt your plans and force you to put your Cruise Moves on hold. Research shows that only 25 percent of evening exercisers consistently do their exercise routines, compared to 75 per-cent of morning exercisers.

The bottom line is that when you commit to exercising in the morning, you bypass excuses and shed the pounds and lose inches faster because you are more con-sistent.

Here are some more wonderful benefits for morning exercise:

• Starting your day with Cruise Moves helps to put you in a fit-ness state of mind. When you feel good about your morning efforts, you'll want to continue your good habits all day long. That means you'll make better food choices almost automatically!

• A study from Indiana Univer-sity in Bloomington suggests that morning workouts reduce blood pressure more than workouts done at other times during the day. In fact, morning exercisers experienced an eight-point drop in systolic pressure (top number)

---

your "8 minute" edge

By exercising in the morning you will:

1. Dramatically boost your metabolism

2. Experience an endor-phin high that will make you feel great

3. Ensure you consistently lose 2 pounds a week

that lasted 11 hours. Their diastolic pressure (bottom number) dropped six points for up to 4 hours after exercise. Evening exercisers showed no significant reductions.

• Doing your Cruise Moves in the morning helps you create muscle faster. Resting levels of testosterone, the body's primary muscle-building hormone, are the highest in the morning. This suggests that the muscle-building potential of resistance training may be at its peak before noon.

the power of rest

If you take a look at the schedule on page 50, you'll notice that each weekend you have time off from your Cruise Moves. Use this time to rest, recover, and enjoy all of the new changes taking place in your body. On Saturdays, I strongly suggest you help your body rejuvenate from your week of hard work with a cleansing ritual (which I'll explain shortly). I encourage you to spend your weekends rewarding yourself for your efforts. Go out and buy a new outfit that shows off your belly or take your new, stronger body for a walk in the park. Allow

How to Get Up for Your Morning Moves

Are you a morning person? Some people are, some aren't. But if you think of yourself as a "night owl," know that you can still benefit from doing your Cruise Moves in the morning. In fact, whether you are a morning or evening person isn't so much as matter of genetics as it is as matter of your mindset and lifestyle. I know, because I used to hate getting up in the morning. But I began telling myself that I was a morning person and going to bed earlier. Now, with enough rest, I can spring right out of bed feeling refreshed!

Here are some ways to help yourself get up for your Cruise Moves.

Say, "I'm a morning person." As I've said, if you believe you are a morning person, you will become a morning person. Our thoughts are powerful and control our actions. Change your thoughts, and your actions will soon follow.

Let the sun wake you up. Sunlight governs our natural sleep-wake cycles. Artificial lighting, however, tends to throw off this natural cycle, allowing us to feel alert at night when the world's natural darkness would otherwise signal our brains to feel sleepy. Artificially darkened rooms also throw off this cycle, making us feel tired in the morning when natural sunlight would wake us up.

Stop pulling your shades down when you go to bed at night. That way, your room will become lighter and lighter as the sun rises, and you'll already be awake and alert long before your alarm clock sounds.

Go a little at a time. Your body has a set internal clock, so at first, you'll have a hard time falling asleep an hour or more earlier than you're used to. Start by changing your bedtime by just 15 minutes. Then, when you're used to that, add another 15, and then another 15, until you're going to bed an hour earlier.

yourself to relax in a warm bubble bath. This is your time. Relish it.

Indeed, rest and relaxation may be one of the most important secrets to creating lean muscle tissue!

Here's why rest is so important. First, your muscles need a minimum of 48 hours of rest between resistance-training sessions in order to repair themselves and grow. It's actually during the resting phase that the true magic happens. If you don't allow your muscles enough rest between Cruise Move sessions, they will remain weak. In fact, you can even injure yourself!

That's why my program requires you to focus on a different area of the body each day of the week. I always provide your muscles with at least 48 hours of rest between sessions. This is why you target your abdomen only on Mondays, Wednesdays, and Fridays. The break on Tuesdays and Thursdays allows your abdominal muscles to recover and strengthen themselves.

But you need more than just downtime. You also need to get a good night's sleep. It's during sleep, particularly deep, stage 4 sleep that your body repairs and regenerates itself. During stage 4 sleep, your body secretes growth hormone, a protein used to repair muscles and injured tissues.

If you don't spend enough time in stage 4 sleep, this important body repair process doesn't fully complete itself.

In fact, researchers suspect that people who have chronic pain syndromes like fibromyalgia don't spend enough time in stage 4 sleep. In experiments done in the 1970s, it took just a week of light sleeping—where people were not allowed to enter stage 4 sleep—before muscle aches and pains popped up.

Other research has found that getting just 1 hour too little of sleep can lower levels of the hormone testosterone. Though more abundant in men, both men and women have this hormone, important in the muscle-creating process. When you don't have enough testosterone, it throws off your muscle-to-fat ratio, promoting fat storage and hindering muscle development.

Also, when you don't sleep enough, your body overproduces the stress hormone cortisol. This not only makes you jumpy and grumpy, but also directs fat storage to your belly and turns up your hunger! In addition, the hormone insulin fails to work properly, not fully shuttling sugar into cells. This makes you feel tired, encourages fat storage, and makes you hungrier than normal.

Some studies have linked sleep

"Try taking a warm bath before bed to soothe away stressful thoughts or tension that might be keeping you awake."

loss to overeating. Research shows that the later people stay up at night, the more likely they are to overeat. And when you crave late-night munchies, are you really going to reach for something healthful? A study done in Japan found that those who had the fewest hours of sleep tended to eat the fewest amounts of vegetables.

If you get too little sleep, you will snack more during the day, using food to help you stay alert. Lack of sleep also affects your levels of leptin, the hormone that decreases your appetite. When levels are low, you crave sweets and starches. Finally, a study done on men who suffer from sleep apnea—a condition that causes you to stop breathing and wake repeatedly throughout the night—found that fatigue resulting from lost sleep made men less likely to exercise and made exercise feel more difficult.

Not getting enough sleep can also cause depression and bad moods, which can lead to overeating. It also lowers your immunity, which can lead to colds that force you to skip your Cruise Moves sessions. Finally, when you go to bed on time, you're more likely to get out of bed on time— in time to do your Cruise Moves.

Surveys show that only about one-third of people sleep at least 8 hours. Promise me that you will make sleep a priority. Turn off the TV and head to bed at a reasonable hour. Your body will thank you. Even an extra hour of sleep will help to reset your body clock, allowing you to wake up refreshed and rejuvenated and ready to face your Cruise Moves.

In addition to rest and sleep, you also need plenty of relaxation. Too often we lead very busy, very stressed lives. This hectic pace can make it hard to see the big picture about what's most important—*your health*. Giving yourself a weekly relaxation period—some time just for you—can help you take a step back to focus on what's most important. It can also help you lower your stress levels. As I mentioned in chapter 2, high levels of stress hormones have been linked with belly fat.

I recommend that you find a way to relax on the weekends that works for you. Some people like to meditate, others like to take long walks, and others like to laugh with friends. Make the most of your relaxation time and don't allow yourself to feel guilty. You're working hard during the week. You need the weekend to rest and ready yourself for the following week of Cruise Moves!

the builder of your best body

So now you know the first essential step to creating a firm belly. I hope you will commit yourself to carving out 8 minutes a day to do your Cruise Moves. Once you do so, I'm confident that you will never go back to another belly or

abs program. You will get so addicted to the ease and powerful weight-loss results of Cruise Moves that you'll join my millions of online clients and become a *Jorge Cruise® client* for life!

"An extra hour of sleep will help to reset your body clock, allowing you to wake up refreshed and rejuvenated and ready to face your Cruise Moves."

Chapter 5

Putting the Jorge Cruise® Plan into Action

Three Different Levels of Challenge, One Flat Belly

getting started

Welcome to your *8 Minutes in the Morning for a Perfect Body* program! Now is the time for you to start your beautiful belly journey.

In the following pages, you'll find three different programs, ranging in difficulty from gentle to challenging.

Start with Level 1, the gentlest of the programs. Each program starts on a Monday and ends on a Sunday. You'll follow each program for 3 weeks before moving on to the next level. In other words, you'll start Level 1 on a Monday and follow it for 21 days, starting over each Monday. After 21 days, you'll advance to Level 2. After 21 more days, you'll advance to Level 3.

If you are already fairly fit, Level 1 may be too easy for you. If you don't feel challenged by the exercises, move up to Level 2 after just 1 week.

a two-step format

Each day of each level follows the same simple format. Each day you'll find:

Step 1. 8 Minutes of Cruise Moves

Step 2. An Eat Nutritionally, *Not* Emotionally visualization

step 1. 8 minutes of cruise moves

During your Monday through Friday sessions, you will find four different Cruise Moves. Your sessions Monday, Wednesday, and Friday will focus on your belly. Your Tuesday sessions will target your upper body, and your Thursday sessions your lower body. Before your Cruise Moves, warm up by jogging or marching in place for a minute or two. **Do each Cruise Move for 1 minute and then go on to the next one. After you've completed all four moves, repeat each move one time for a total of 8 minutes.** Then cool down with the stretches suggested on the opposite page.

Note: You'll take each weekend off from your Cruise Moves, but not from building lean muscle and taking additional steps toward your goal. Each Saturday you will do a body cleanse as described on pages 170–171. Each Sunday you will record your progress by weighing yourself and taking your waist measurements.

your "8 minute" edge

During each week of your *8 Minutes in the Morning for a Perfect Body* journey, you will:

• Feel your abdominal muscles become tighter, firmer, and stronger

• Lose 2 pounds of fat

Your Warmup and Cooldown

Before your Cruise Moves, I recommend that you simply jog in place for 1 minute to help increase your body temperature so that you are limber and loose. This will help you avoid any injuries. After your Cruise Moves, do the following stretches to cool down and increase your flexibility.

Sky-reaching pose. Stand tall and reach with both hands toward the sky as high as you comfortably can. Feel the stretch lengthening your spine, bringing more range of motion to your joints. Breathe deeply through your nose. Hold from 10 seconds to 1 minute.

Hurdler's stretch. Sit on a towel or mat on the floor with your legs extended in front of you. Keeping your back straight, gently bend forward from the hips and reach as far as you can toward your toes. If possible, pull your toes back slightly toward your upper body. Again, don't worry if this stretch is difficult for you right now—do the best you can. Eventually, you'll get it! Hold from 10 seconds to 1 minute.

Cobra stretch. Lie on a towel or mat on your belly with your palms flat on the ground next to your shoulders and your legs just slightly less than shoulder-width apart. Your feet should be resting on their tops. Lift your upper body up off the ground, inhaling through your nose as you rise. Press your hips into the floor and curve your upper body backward, looking up. This stretch is one that you may need to work up to, so right now, do the best you can. Hold from 10 seconds to 1 minute.

your current body and future goals

To find your healthy weight, find your age and height on the chart below, selecting a number that is realistic for you. Subtract that number from your current weight. That's your weight-loss goal. To determine a target date for achieving this goal, divide your goal weight by two. That's the number of weeks it will take to reach your goal. Consult a calendar and find the date you will achieve your goal weight.

Please record your answers to the following:

your current body

1. What is your current weight? _____

2. What is your current waist circumference in inches? _____

your future body

1. What is your goal weight? _____

2. What is your goal waist circumference in inches? _____

3. Date I will achieve my goal: _____

4. List any other goals: _____

your weight chart

Height (ft/in.)	Weight (lb) 19–34 yr	35+ yr	Height (ft/in.)	Weight (lb) 19–34 yr	35+ yr
5'0"	97–128	108–38	5'8"	125–64	138–78
5'1"	101–32	111–43	5'9"	129–69	142–83
5'2"	104–37	115–48	5'10"	132–74	146–88
5'3"	107–41	119–52	5'11"	136–79	151–94
5'4"	111–46	122–57	6'0"	140–84	155–99
5'5"	114–50	126–62	6'1"	144–89	159–205
5'6"	118–55	130–67	6'2"	148–95	164–210
5'7"	121–60	134–72	6'3"	152–200	168–216

SOURCE: U.S. Department of Health and Human Services, Dietary Guidelines for Americans

step 2: eat nutritionally, *not* emotionally

Each morning I'll provide you with a powerful visualization to help you overcome emotional eating and stay motivated. Your mind can lead your body to do amazing things. Studies have shown how powerful this mind-body connection is. For example, when athletes visualize sprinting to the finish line and winning a race, the muscle fibers in their legs can actually start twitching as if they were actually running. When you create an image in your mind of what you want to accomplish, you take the first crucial step to making your dreams a reality. Indeed, visualizing yourself with a beautiful belly will help you create a firm belly. What's more, visualizing yourself doing all the necessary tasks to create a beautiful belly—such as your Cruise Moves—will help you to stay focused and motivated. Finally, you can also use the power of visualization to help overcome negative emotions that may be driving you to overeat.

During your visualizations, you need to draw on all of your senses: touch, taste, smell, sight, and sound. The more senses you involve in your visualizations, the more powerful your images will become and the more effective your time spent.

a power thought

In addition to your visualization and Cruise Moves, I've also provided you with a power thought for each day of your program, designed to help you maximize your success. They will provide you with additional ways to optimize muscle restoration as well as inspirational help for sticking with the program.

your homework

Before you get started on your new adventure, you'll need to make sure you have the tools for the journey. Please don't start the program until you do the following.

1. Purchase your equipment. You will need a medicine ball and large, air-filled fitness ball (also called a Swiss ball). These are available at most sporting goods stores. You can use a basketball in place of the medicine ball, but you will get the best results with a real medicine ball. Visit www.jorgecruise.com/bellytools for online links to some of the brands of balls that I personally recommend.

2. Read chapters 1 through 3. Please don't start the program without first reading about how it works and understanding the formula behind the two-step process.

3. Purchase the psyllium shakes that you will drink each Saturday morning. Visit www.jorgecruise.com to visit my online shop to purchase psyllium husks powder.

4. Write down your current weight and measurements and take a "before" photo. Your original weight, waist circumference, and before photo will not only help serve as powerful reminders of your goal, but they will also help you to see your progress. To take your measurements, use a flexible tape measure. Wrap it around your waist, just above your hipbones. Record your answers in the space provided on the following page.

MY "BEFORE" AND "AFTER" PHOTOS

Your "before" and "after" photos will help motivate you to stay focused on your weight-loss goal.
Review this page each day to *prevent* emotional eating. Take your "before" photo
right now and paste it on this page. But don't wait to see your future body!
Go to www.jorgecruise.com/futurebody and print out your "after" photo right now.
Photocopy this page for each day of the program and use it to keep yourself organized.

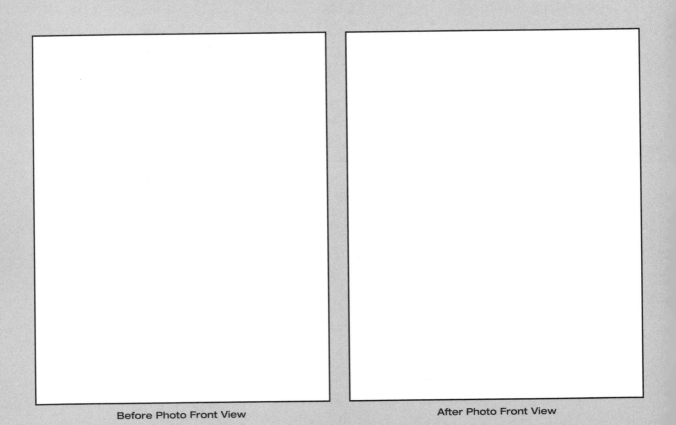

Before Photo Front View   **After Photo Front View**

Instructions for using the planner: Make seven copies for each week. Then stack them and staple in the upper left-hand corner. Keep them with you at all times.

JORGE CRUISE®
FLAT BELLY PLANNER

Date _____

Step 1: 8 Minute Moves®

Muscle-Making Routine:

Monday: Belly Day
Tuesday: Upper Body
Wednesday: Belly Day
Thursday: Lower Body
Friday: Belly Day
Saturday: Body Cleanse
Sunday: Day Off

	Set 1	Set 2
Move 1:		
Move 2:		
Move 3:		
Move 4:		

In each "Move" box, write down the Cruise Move® and then in the "Set 1 and Set 2" box, keep track of the number of reps performed or time held.

Step 2: Eat Nutritionally, *Not* Emotionally®

Muscle-Making Material:

Veggies: Salad, Steamed Veggies, or 1 Fruit
Fat: 1 tsp of Flax, Olive Oil, or Butter
Carbs: ½ cup of a grain or 1 slice of bread
Protein: 1 oz of Fish/Chicken/Meat/Cheese,
   3 Egg Whites, ½ cup of Beans, or 1 Glass of 1% Milk
Snacks: 100-calorie Item
Treat: 30- to 50-calorie Item

Each box equals an above example. eat every 3 hours and stop eating 3 hours before bed.

Breakfast

- Veggies/Fruit _____ ☐
- Fat _____ ☐
- Carbs _____ ☐
- Protein _____ ☐☐☐

Snack _____ ☐

Lunch

- Veggies/Fruit _____ ☐
- Fat _____ ☐
- Carbs _____ ☐
- Protein _____ ☐☐☐

Snack _____ ☐

Dinner

- Veggies/Fruit _____ ☐
- Fat _____ ☐
- Carbs _____ ☐
- Protein _____ ☐☐☐
- Treat _____ ☐

Water (✔): 8-oz Glass

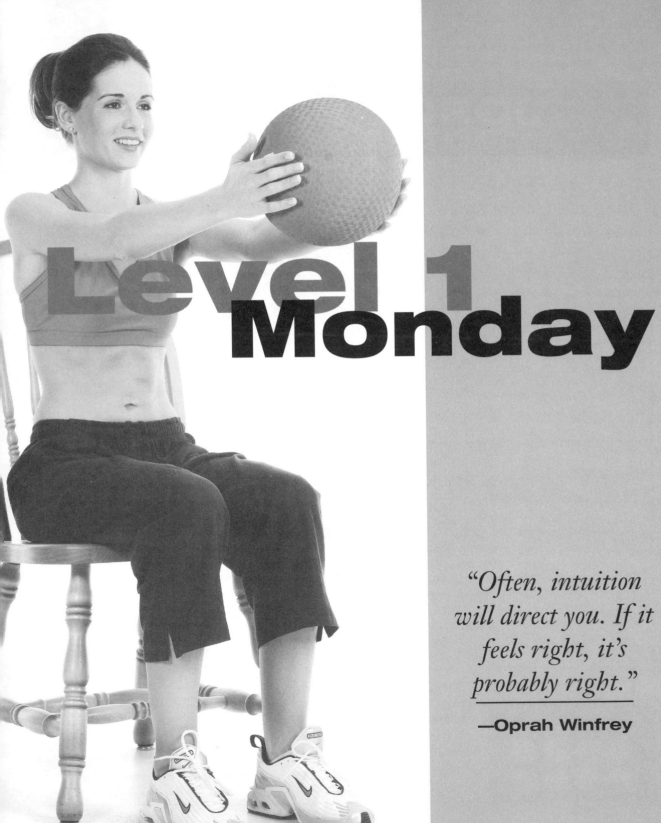

Level 1
Monday

> "Often, intuition will direct you. If it feels right, it's probably right."
>
> —Oprah Winfrey

jorge's power thought

Many people ask me whether they can skip their cooldown stretches. They tell me that stretching won't help them create a beautiful belly, so why bother? Well, that's simply not true. Stretching helps you accomplish your goal in a number of ways. Most important, stretching helps increase *flexibility*, which in turn, helps your muscles to grow stronger. Yes, it's true! Researchers have found that flexible muscles tend to be stronger and more aerobic than tight muscles. **Stretching will also help to lengthen your muscles, creating a long, lean appearance.** Finally, it helps to bring circulation to your muscles, allowing them to recover more quickly from your Cruise Moves. So after each 8-minute routine, do your best to squeeze in my three cooldown stretches.

"With visualization, what you see is what you get. Visualizing your future helps you make your results a reality."

8 minute moves®
belly day

MOVE 1: seated vacuum
transverse abdominus

a. Sit in a sturdy chair with your feet flat on the floor. As you exhale, suck your navel in toward your spine as far as you can, contracting your belly to squeeze all of the air out of your lungs. Hold for 1 to 3 seconds.

b. Inhale as you reverse the exercise, this time making your belly as round as possible. Continue exhaling and inhaling slowly for 1 minute, then move on to Move 2.

a

b

8-MINUTE LOG				
exercise	move 1	move 2	move 3	move 4
sets				
reps				

MOVE 2: seated crossover
upper rectus abdominus

a. Remain seated with your feet flat on the floor. Sit tall with a long spine. Bend your arms 90 degrees, bringing your elbows in line with your chest, your forearms perpendicular to the floor, and your fingers toward the ceiling.

b. Exhale as you bring your left elbow and right knee toward one another. Inhale as you bring your elbow and knee back to the starting position. Repeat with your right elbow and left knee, alternating between those positions for 1 minute. After 1 minute move on to Move 3 on page 66.

a

b

exercise sequence

1. warm up Jog or march in place for 1 minute.

2. cruise moves Do one 60-second repetition of each of your 4 Cruise Moves. Repeat this cycle and you will be done in 8 minutes.

3. cool down After your Cruise Moves, do these stretches (see page 57).

Sky-reaching pose | **Hurdler's stretch** | **Cobra stretch**

belly day (cont'd)

MOVE 3: seated torso rotation
obliques

a. Remain seated with your feet flat on the floor. Sit tall with a long spine. Grasp your medicine ball (or a bag of flour) at chest level, with your arms extended.

b. Remain erect as you exhale and twist to the right. Keep your head and neck in line with your torso as you twist so that you are always facing the ball. Try not to lean forward. Inhale as you return to the starting position and then repeat on the other side. Continue for 1 minute, then move on to Move 4.

a

b

eat nutritionally, *not* emotionally®
visualization

To make sure you eat "nutritionally" and not "emotionally," you can use a powerful mind-body technique called visualization to help you stay emotionally strong and empowered. Too often, we use the power of visualization somewhat unconsciously, in a negative way. We focus on negative concepts about life, which only works to fulfill that negative vision. So today and for the rest of your Level 1 moves, we're going to do the opposite. You will focus on the beautiful belly you want to create, using the power of visualization to help you make your goal a reality.

MOVE 4: captain's chair
lower rectus abdominus

a. Remain seated with your feet flat on the floor. Sit tall with a long spine. Grasp the edge of the chair with your fingers on either side of your hips. Reach your palms into the chair to add stability to your torso.

b. Exhale as you slowly bring your knees toward your chest, trying not to arch your lower back as you do so. Hold for 1 to 3 seconds and then slowly lower as you inhale. Repeat for 1 minute, then return to Move 1 on page 64. Repeat Moves 1–4 once more, and you're done.

a

b

see your beautiful belly

Do the following visualization exercise with me for just a few minutes. Close your eyes and take a few relaxing breaths—in through your nose and out through your mouth. Smile and jump into the future with me. Visualize the day that you reach your goal.

See yourself jump out of bed and complete your Cruise Moves. Then while planning your day, notice

your belly. How does it look? Touch your belly with your hands. How does it feel to have a flat belly?

Get dressed, making sure to pick an outfit you've always wanted to wear, but couldn't because of your belly. Notice that your clothes feel loose around your belly. Notice how flat your belly looks in this outfit. Smile. You've reached your goal!

Level 1
Tuesday

"Never look where you're going. Always look where you want to go."

—Bob Ernst

jorge's power thought

As I told you on pages 52–53, you must get enough sleep to allow your muscles to repair themselves. Did you know that a solid night's sleep can also sharpen your mind and lift your spirits? That's right, simply getting enough Zzz's makes concentration easier and even improves your ability to learn. This is because the more sleep you get, the more minutes your brain spends in the rapid-eye movement (REM) phase of sleep. And REM sleep is crucial for cementing new information into long- and short-term memory. Research suggests that it is during REM sleep that we file away everything we learn. So promise me that you will hit the sack at a reasonable hour tonight.

"The more senses you use, the more effective your visualization. See, hear, smell, feel, touch, and taste your future."

8 minute moves®
upper-body day

MOVE 1: wall pumps
chest

a. Stand arm's length away from a wall with your feet under your hips. Lean forward and place your palms against the wall with your fingers pointing up. Your arms should be extended with only a slight bend in your elbows.

b. Inhale as you slowly bend your elbows, bringing your chest and torso closer to the wall. Keep your abdominals firm and your back long and straight throughout. Exhale as you slowly press yourself back to the starting position, straightening your arms as you go. Repeat for 1 minute and then move on to Move 2.

a

b

8-MINUTE LOG				
exercise	move 1	move 2	move 3	move 4
sets				
reps				

MOVE 2: sleepwalker hold
shoulders

a. Stand with your feet under your hips, your abs firm, and your back long and straight. Exhale as you raise your arms in front of your torso to shoulder level. Make sure to keep your shoulders relaxed away from your ears. Hold for 1 minute as you breathe normally, then move on to Move 3 on page 72.

a

exercise sequence

1. warm up Jog or march in place for 1 minute.

2. cruise moves Do one 60-second repetition of each of your 4 Cruise Moves. Repeat this cycle and you will be done in 8 minutes.

3. cool down After your Cruise Moves, do these stretches (see page 57).

Sky-reaching pose | Hurdler's stretch | Cobra stretch

upper-body day (cont'd)

MOVE 3: lift hold
biceps

a. Sit about 2 feet in front of a table in a sturdy chair (one without wheels) with your feet flat on the floor. Place your palms under the tabletop with your elbows bent about 90 degrees. Push up on the underside of the table as hard as you can. Hold for 1 minute as you breathe normally, then move on to Move 4.

a

eat nutritionally, *not* emotionally®
visualization

To truly visualize the new you, you must feel relaxed and calm. Your mind should be free of mental clutter to allow yourself to better focus on your visualization. If you are not in a relaxed state, negative thoughts may pop up. But being relaxed allows the message to affect you more powerfully. So before today's visualization, I want you to go to a quiet room in your house, play some soft music, and do whatever you need to do to relax.

MOVE 4: push down hold
triceps

b. Remain seated in front of the table and place your palms on the table top with your elbows bent about 90 degrees. Exhale as you press down into the table as hard as you can. Hold for up to 60 seconds, breathing normally. Then return to Move 1 on page 70. Repeat Moves 1–4 once more, and you're done.

b

noticing the small stuff

Today, I want you to jump into the future again and visualize yourself after you meet your goal. First, focus your visualization on your belly. Then, notice your entire body. See how fit and firm your arms have become. Notice your vibrant skin. Visualize how your clothes will fall on your body and how your shoes will fit. Imagine the colors, textures, and patterns of a favorite outfit that you will be wearing. What does the new you look like? Will you have a new haircut, new makeup, or new accessories? See your body doing different movements. See yourself walking, sitting at work, or driving in your car. Try to visualize every detail. You have to smell, hear, touch, and taste your vision to make it a reality.

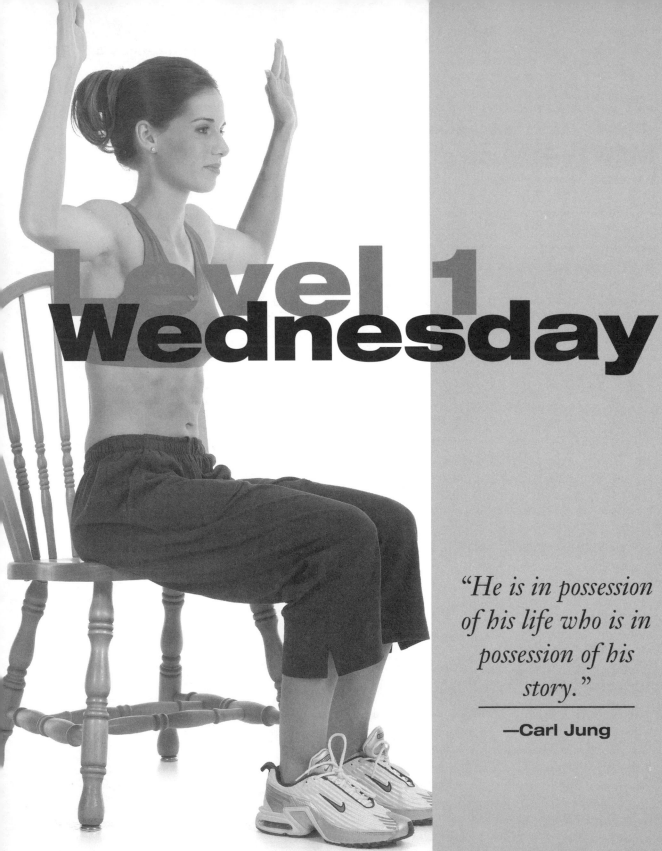

Level 1
Wednesday

"He is in possession of his life who is in possession of his story."

—Carl Jung

jorge's power thought

Vitamin C plays a very important role in muscle recovery after your Cruise Moves. This important vitamin helps produce collagen, which is a connective tissue that holds muscles, bones, and other tissues together. During your Cruise Moves, as your breathing increases to meet the demands of your workout, the chemical interaction of oxygen with your cell membranes, protein, and other cellular components creates damaging substances called free radicals. These free radicals are highly reactive substances that, much like small fires, must be extinguished before they burn, or "oxidize" neighboring molecules in other cells, creating muscle soreness and stiffness. Vitamin C is a dietary antioxidant that helps to put out free radical damage in and around your cells. So my tip to you is to take a vitamin C supplement every day—ideally, 1,000 milligrams.

"I'm so proud of you for committing to this journey. Congratulate yourself. The first few steps are often the hardest steps you'll take in your journey to a new you."

8 minute moves®
belly day

MOVE 1: seated vacuum
transverse abdominus

a. Sit in a sturdy chair with your feet flat on the floor. As you exhale, suck your navel in toward your spine as far as you can, contracting your belly to squeeze all of the air out of your lungs. Hold for 1 to 3 seconds.

b. Inhale as you reverse the exercise, this time making your belly as round as possible. Continue exhaling and inhaling slowly for 1 minute, then move on to the next Cruise Move 2.

a

b

8-MINUTE LOG				
exercise	move 1	move 2	move 3	move 4
sets				
reps				

MOVE 2: seated crossover
upper rectus abdominus

a. Remain seated with your feet flat on the floor. Sit tall with a long spine. Bend your arms 90 degrees, bringing your elbows in line with your chest, your forearms perpendicular to the floor, and your fingers toward the ceiling.

b. Exhale as you bring your left elbow and right knee toward one another. Inhale as you bring your elbow and knee back to the starting position. Repeat with your right elbow and left knee, alternating between those positions for 1 minute. After 1 minute move on to Move 3 on page 78.

a

b

exercise sequence

1. warm up Jog or march in place for 1 minute.

2. cruise moves Do one 60-second repetition of each of your 4 Cruise Moves. Repeat this cycle and you will be done in 8 minutes.

3. cool down After your Cruise Moves, do these stretches (see page 57).

Sky-reaching pose | **Hurdler's stretch** | **Cobra stretch**

belly day (cont'd)

MOVE 3: seated torso rotation
obliques

a. Remain seated with your feet flat on the floor. Sit tall with a long spine. Grasp your medicine ball at chest level, with your arms extended.

b. Remain erect as you exhale and twist to the right. Keep your head and neck in line with your torso as you twist so that you are always facing the ball. Try not to lean forward. Inhale as you return to the starting position and then repeat on the other side. Continue for 1 minute, then move on to Move 4.

a

b

eat nutritionally, *not* emotionally®
visualization

As we've done for the past 2 days, today we'll take another look into the future. You will visualize a day after you've reached your goal. Today, you're preparing for a very special date! So, first relax by closing your eyes and taking a few deep, relaxing breaths, in through your nose and out through your mouth. Allow each exhalation to bring you to a state of deep relaxation. Once you feel completely relaxed, you're ready to begin.

MOVE 4: captain's chair
lower rectus abdominus

a. Remain seated with your feet flat on the floor. Sit tall with a long spine. Grasp the edge of the chair with your fingers on either side of your hips. Reach your palms into the chair to add stability to your torso.

b. Exhale as you slowly bring your knees toward your chest, trying not to arch your lower back as you do so. Hold for 1 to 3 seconds and then slowly lower as you inhale. Repeat for 1 minute, then return to Move 1 on page 76. Repeat Moves 1–4 once more, and you're done.

a

b

your first date

See yourself getting ready for your date. Who will be your date for the evening? How do you prepare for your date? See yourself taking a hot bubble bath with a glass of sparkling water or splurging on a facial. Then, pick out your outfit. Find an outfit that you've always loved but one that you refused to wear because of your belly. Put it on. See how flat your belly

looks in this outfit! Notice how the fabric touches against your toned skin. Look in the mirror and twirl around and smile at how slim and healthy you look.

Hear the doorbell ring. Open the door and see your date. Hear your date comment about at how lovely you look. What does your date say and how does it make you feel?

Level 1
Thursday

"*Health is beauty, and the most perfect health is the most perfect beauty.*"

—**William Shenstone**

jorge's power thought

You need protein to help create new lean muscle, and fish is one of the best protein sources around. Besides quality protein, certain types of cold-water fatty fish contain a special type of fat called omega-3 fatty acids. These special fats have been shown to help reduce muscle soreness after a workout. They also help to boost your mood, turn down your appetite, and give your skin a radiant glow. What type of fish should you eat? I recommend you stick with salmon. This type of fish is very rich in omega-3 fatty acids. Also, according to the Environmental Protection Agency, it's least likely to contain contaminants such as PCBs and mercury, making salmon safe for pregnant and nursing women.

"Be good to yourself. Try to stop those negative thoughts that tell you that you are not good enough. You are worth it."

8 minute moves®
lower-body day

MOVE 1: superman hold
lower back

a. Stand in front of a sturdy chair. Your right foot should be directly under your right hip. Bend forward and place your right palm on the chair's seat, just under your right shoulder. Exhale as you raise and extend your left leg back and your left arm forward, forming a straight line from foot to fingertips. Do not lock your elbow or knee. Hold for up to 30 seconds, breathing normally, then repeat on the other side. Release and move to Move 2.

a

8-MINUTE LOG				
exercise	move 1	move 2	move 3	move 4
sets				
reps				

MOVE 2: squat pump
quadriceps

a. Stand with your feet hip-width apart. Place your hands on your hips. Check your posture. Make sure your back is long and straight, your shoulders are relaxed away from your ears, and your abdominals are firm.

b. Inhale as you bend your knees and squat no more than 90 degrees. (Squat only as deeply as you feel comfortable.) Make sure your knees remain over your ankles (not over your toes). Keep your abs firm and your back straight. Exhale as you press up slowly to the starting position. Repeat for 60 seconds, then move on to Move 3 on page 84.

a

b

exercise sequence

1. warm up Jog or march in place for 1 minute.

2. cruise moves Do one 60-second repetition of each of your 4 Cruise Moves. Repeat this cycle and you will be done in 8 minutes.

3. cool down After your Cruise Moves, do these stretches (see page 57).

Sky-reaching pose | **Hurdler's stretch** | **Cobra stretch**

lower-body day (cont'd)

MOVE 3: lift pump
hamstrings

a. Stand about 1 foot in front of a wall with your feet under your hips. Rest your hands against the wall for balance. Check your posture. Make sure your back is long and straight, your shoulders are relaxed away from your ears, and your abs are firm.

b. Exhale as you lift your right foot toward your right buttock. (For added difficulty, use ankle weights.) Stop once you achieve a 90-degree angle. Inhale, lower, and repeat for up to 30 seconds. Repeat with your left leg, then move on to Move 4.

a

b

eat nutritionally, *not* emotionally® visualization

Today is a glorious summer day filled with sunshine and warm breezes. It's the perfect day to hit the beach with a few of your friends during a very relaxing visualization exercise. Close your eyes and take a few relaxing breaths, in through your nose and out through your mouth. Allow each exhalation to bring you to a state of deep relaxation. Once you feel completely relaxed, you're ready to begin.

MOVE 4: standing calf pump
calves

a. Remain standing in front of the wall with your feet under your hips and your arms resting at your sides. Check your posture. Make sure your back is long and straight, your shoulders are relaxed away from your ears, and your abs are firm. Place one hand on the wall for balance. Exhale as you rise onto the balls of your feet, bringing your heels off the floor. Inhale as you lower. Repeat for 60 seconds, then return to Move 1 on page 82. Repeat Moves 1–4 once more, and you're done.

a

your bikini belly

You've decided to spend the day at the beach with some friends. You haven't been to the beach in years since your belly made you feel too embarrassed to wear a swimsuit. But now you've got a beautiful belly, so slip on your swimsuit and wide-brimmed straw hat. Once there, you sink your toes into the hot sand and let out a deep sigh of delight. As you bare down to your bathing suit and spread out on your towel, you feel confident and beautiful. Feel the warm rays on your back. One of your buddies comments on how great you look and you reply with a heartfelt "thank you" and tell her just how great you feel. You spend the afternoon gossiping on your beach towel and frolicking in the waves.

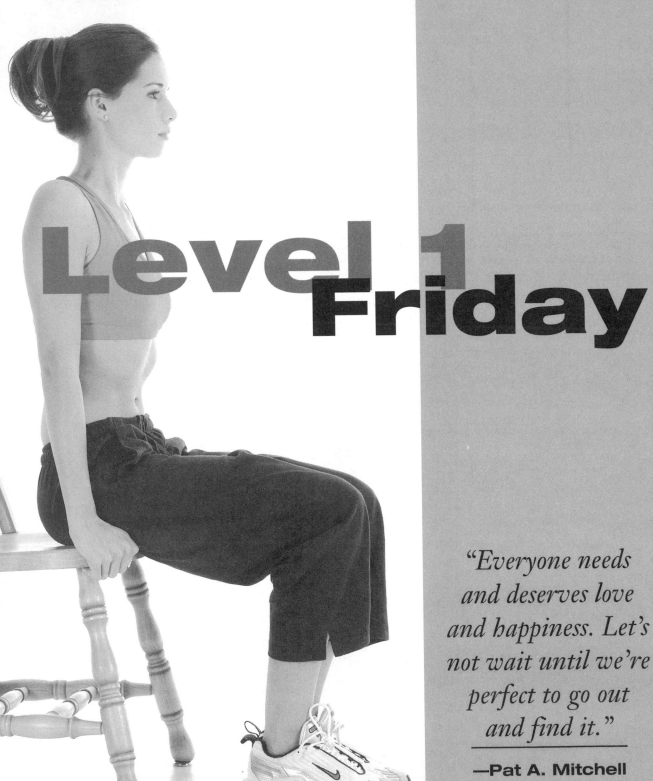

Level 1 Friday

> "Everyone needs and deserves love and happiness. Let's not wait until we're perfect to go out and find it."
>
> —Pat A. Mitchell

jorge's power thought

Have you ever watched a child eat? They eat a bite, squirm around as they chew it, and, of course, play with their food. Plus, they always stop when they've had enough. Is there something we can learn here? You bet! Children listen to the instinctual cues that their bodies send them, so they stop when they're full. If you pay close attention while you eat, you'll notice that the pleasure you get from food tends to diminish as you continue to eat. This is a sign that your body has had enough, but many people eat so fast that they don't notice this signal. *Bring your inner child to the table.* Go ahead and have fun with your food when nobody's looking—and make it last. Make train tracks with your fork in your mashed potatoes; eat your sandwich crust first to make a funny shape. Your dinner will be a lot more fun and you'll probably eat a lot less.

"Don't forget: Your body is the most precious gift you've ever received. Treat it with the respect it deserves."

8 minute moves®
belly day

MOVE 1: seated vacuum
transverse abdominus

a. Sit in a sturdy chair with your feet flat on the floor. As you exhale, suck your navel in toward your spine as far as you can, contracting your belly to squeeze all of the air out of your lungs. Hold for 1 to 3 seconds.

b. Inhale as you reverse the exercise, this time making your belly as round as possible. Continue exhaling and inhaling slowly for 1 minute, then move on to Move 2.

a

b

8-MINUTE LOG				
exercise	move 1	move 2	move 3	move 4
sets				
reps				

MOVE 2: seated crossover
upper rectus abdominus

a. Remain seated with your feet flat on the floor. Sit tall with a long spine. Bend your arms 90 degrees, bringing your elbows in line with your chest, your forearms perpendicular to the floor, and your fingers toward the ceiling.

b. Exhale as you bring your left elbow and right knee toward one another. Inhale as you bring your elbow and knee back to the starting position. Repeat with your right elbow and left knee, alternating between those positions for 1 minute. After 1 minute move on to Move 3 on page 90.

a

b

exercise sequence

1. warm up Jog or march in place for 1 minute.

2. cruise moves Do one 60-second repetition of each of your 4 Cruise Moves. Repeat this cycle and you will be done in 8 minutes.

3. cool down After your Cruise Moves, do these stretches (see page 57).

Sky-reaching pose | Hurdler's stretch | Cobra stretch

belly day (cont'd)

MOVE 3: seated torso rotation
obliques

a. Remain seated with your feet flat on the floor. Sit tall with a long spine. Grasp your medicine ball at chest level, with your arms extended.

b. Remain erect as you exhale and twist to the right. Keep your head and neck in line with your torso as you twist so that you are always facing the ball. Try not to lean forward. Inhale as you return to the starting position and then repeat on the other side. Continue for 1 minute, then move on to Move 4.

a

b

eat nutritionally, *not emotionally*® visualization

Today we will nurture your inner motivation with a very special visualization exercise. During today's visualization, you will be reunited with an old friend who hasn't seen you for many years. So, close your eyes and take a few relaxing breaths, in through your nose and out through your mouth. Allow each exhalation to bring you to a state of deep relaxation. Once you feel completely relaxed, you're ready to begin.

MOVE 4: captain's chair
lower rectus abdominus

a. Remain seated with your feet flat on the floor. Sit tall with a long spine. Grasp the edge of the chair with your fingers on either side of your hips. Reach your palms into the chair to add stability to your torso.

b. Exhale as you slowly bring your knees toward your chest, trying not to arch your lower back as you do so. Hold for 1 to 3 seconds and then slowly lower as you inhale. Repeat for 1 minute, then return to Move 1 on page 88. Repeat Moves 1–4 once more, and you're done.

a

b

seeing an old friend

See yourself pulling into the parking garage at the airport to pick up your friend. Take a look in the rearview mirror—you look healthier, happier, and younger than you have in years! You quickly head to the stairs and mount them two at a time. Feel how strong your body feels as you rapidly climb each staircase. Doesn't it feel wonderful to be able to move quickly without feeling out of breath? You make it to the gate just in time to see your friend approach. She smiles politely, says, "excuse me," and brushes past you. She doesn't recognize you! You call her name and say, "It's me!" Your friend turns around, stunned, and says, "You look incredible! What have you done?" You smile radiantly.

Level 1
Saturday

"Things turn out best for those who make the best of the way things turn out."

—Daniel Considine

jorge's power thought

One of the best ways to pamper yourself is with a massage. Whether you pay a professional or get a massage from a loved one, it has the same effect. The motion of the massage helps to increase circulation to your muscles as well as break up any knots or tense spots. This helps your muscles to recover from your Cruise Moves and prevents soreness. But massage does even more. New research shows that your metabolism gets a boost when you get a massage. So, while you are relaxing on the table, you'll burn up some extra calories without lifting a finger! Also, there's nothing like the sensation of warm touch to help you relax and release all of your emotional worries. Indeed, regular massages are good for body, mind, and soul. Treat yourself to one today. You've earned it!

"Today we'll do a little spring cleaning for the body. You'll cleanse your body, mind, and soul."

body cleanse
day off from cruise moves

Today is your day off from Cruise Moves, but not a day off from the program. Use today to pamper yourself inside and out. Spend some time relaxing—both your mind and body. Read that novel that you've been putting off. Spend some time at the park, writing in the journal provided on the following page. Or take a nap in the afternoon! This is your day to rest, relax, and rejuvenate, your day to completely cleanse your body.

To cleanse your body, follow my three-step plan:

1. Drink your psyllium shake for breakfast. The shake replaces your meal. Don't have anything for breakfast other than your shake. (To purchase psyllium hulk powder, visit www.jorgecruise.com.)

2. Make both lunch and dinner's protein serving non-meat options. See the bonus chapter starting on page 319 for sample vegetable protein meals.

3. Drink eight 16-ounce glasses of water, doubling your usual water intake.

eat nutritionally, *not* emotionally®
visualization

It's time to get dressed up in your finest attire because tonight you are going to shine at a very elegant, formal affair! You are going to wear that little black dress, the one you've kept in the back of your closet for when you had a body to show off. So close your eyes and take a few relaxing breaths, in through your nose and out through your mouth. Allow each exhalation to bring you to a state of deep relaxation. Once you feel completely relaxed, you're ready to begin.

journal

_____ _____
_____ _____
_____ _____
_____ _____
_____ _____
_____ _____
_____ _____
_____ _____
_____ _____
_____ _____
_____ _____
_____ _____
_____ _____
_____ _____
_____ _____
_____ _____
_____ _____
_____ _____

the little black dress

See yourself getting ready for your special occasion. See the black dress hanging in your closet. Take it out of the closet and drape it over the front of your body. Feel yourself growing excited at the prospect of finally wearing it. Lay the dress on your bed and notice every detail about it. Think back to the last time you wore it. How long ago was that? Then pick it up and slip it on. Feel the silky material fall evenly over your body. Put on your shoes and take a look at yourself in the mirror. See your belly, how nothing bulges. Then, fast forward to your big event. See yourself in the ballroom. Sense all of the eyes on you. You are confident and stunning. Dance the night away and enjoy it!

Level 1
Sunday

"*Energy and persistence conquer all things.*"

—**Benjamin Franklin**

jorge's power thought

I'm sure you've noticed how much better you feel throughout the day after you do your Cruise Moves in the morning. That's not the half of it. Psychologists and exercise physiologists have found that exercise may actually work as well as drugs for treating depression. A study done at Duke University recently tested this theory. They recruited 156 men and women age 50 and older who suffered from major depression. One group walked or jogged for 30 minutes 3 days a week, while another group took the antidepressant Zoloft. At the end of 4 months, both groups had improved dramatically. When the researchers checked back 6 months later to see how the people were faring on their own, 38 percent of the Zoloft group had fallen back into depression, but only 8 percent of the exercise group saw their symptoms return.

"Even God rested on the seventh day. Don't feel guilty. Rest will help to make you stronger."

capture your progress
day off from cruise moves

Today is your day off. Take a moment to relish your progress. Grab a pen and answer the following questions. Then share the answers with me by sending an e-mail to flatbelly1@jorgecruise.com.

1. What is your current weight?

_____

2. What was your original weight?

_____

3. What is your waist circumference in inches?

_____

4. What was your original waist circumference in inches?

_____

5. What have you done well this week? What are you most proud of?

_____

_____

_____

_____

_____

6. What could you improve next week?

_____

_____

_____

_____

_____

eat nutritionally, *not* emotionally® visualization

Today you will take a trip back to high school, seeing all of the high school buddies that you haven't seen in years. It's time for your high school reunion, and you can't wait to show off your new, beautiful belly for all to see. So close your eyes and take a few relaxing breaths, in through your nose and out through your mouth. Allow each exhalation to bring you to a state of deep relaxation. Once you feel completely relaxed, you're ready to begin.

sharon lawson's belly shrank 4 inches!

"This program is so easy. I am not a gym person and have trouble getting motivated to do any exercise in the afternoon or evening. To get up in the morning just a few minutes earlier than usual to tone my belly (a particularly needy area for me) and see results in just a few weeks is a real motivator. The inches I have lost have come from all the right places!

"My results have changed my life. I have more control over my eating habits and the shape and size of my body. I now know that if I follow some basic steps, I can lose the weight, and more important, keep it off over the long haul. I have kept my weight steady for 6 months. I enjoy shopping for clothes and feel that I really look great when I go out. I now choose closer-fitting dresses instead of the looser ones—because I can show off my tummy!"

At age 53, Sharon exchanged her size-10 pants for a size 6!

your reunion

You are excited to show off what has become of you—how slim, healthy, and happy you are! It's time to get dressed. Imagine what you are wearing, what shoes you slip on your feet, what jewelry you put on, how you style your hair, what makeup you apply, and how you feel when you look in the mirror. You look great and feel fabulous!

As you approach the entrance to the reunion, take a deep breath and then confidently glide into the room. Whom do you see from high school and what do they say to you? Hear the compliments and "oohs" and "ahs." Tell your classmates how terrific you feel. Later in the evening, a class picture is taken. See yourself, standing tall, lean, and confident amongst your high school classmates.

Level 2
Monday

"There is always room for improvement, you know—it's the biggest room in the house."

—Louise Heath Leber

jorge's power thought

Are you still dragging yourself out of bed every morning and sluggishly performing your Cruise Moves? Here's a way to jump-start your motivation to move! As soon as your eyes open, bring your hands together for a strong clap. Continue clapping with each breath as you sit up and step out of bed. Make each clap louder and stronger.

Here's why it works. The palms of your hands have more nerve receptors than almost any other part of your body. Clapping your hands will create a neurological jolt that will stimulate your brain and make you feel alive and powerful. Follow up with a few deep, invigorating breaths. Then, jog to the bathroom to brush your teeth. Jogging will further increase the rate of oxygen to your body by causing your heart to pump more blood. By the time you get into position for your Cruise Moves, you'll already be fully alert and ready to conquer the day!

"You've come a long way! Give yourself a big pat on the back. You deserve it."

8 minute moves®
belly day

MOVE 1: vacuum on knees
transverse abdominus

a. Kneel on the floor in a table position with your hands under your shoulders and your knees under your hips. Make sure your spine remains in a neutral position.

b. Exhale as you bring your belly button in toward your spine and contract your abdominal muscles. Bring your belly as far inward as it will go. Hold for 1 to 3 seconds, then exhale and expand your belly as much as it will expand. Continue alternating slowly between the two positions for 1 minute, then move on to Move 2.

a

b

8-MINUTE LOG				
exercise	move 1	move 2	move 3	move 4
sets				
reps				

MOVE 2: plank
rectus abdomimus

a. Lie on your belly with your legs extended. Bend your arms and place your forearms against the floor with your elbows under your shoulders.

a

b. Exhale as you lift your torso into a modified push-up position. Only the balls of your feet and your hands and forearms should touch the floor. Try to form a straight line from your heels to your head, using the strength of your belly to prevent your hips from sagging down toward the floor. Breathe normally as you hold this move. Eventually you want to hold this move for 1 minute, but at first you may only be able to manage 10 seconds. Hold for as long as you can, then move on to Move 3 on page 104.

b

exercise sequence

1. warm up Jog or march in place for 1 minute.

2. cruise moves Do one 60-second repetition of each of your 4 Cruise Moves. Repeat this cycle and you will be done in 8 minutes.

3. cool down After your Cruise Moves, do these stretches (see page 57).

Sky-reaching pose | **Hurdler's stretch** | **Cobra stretch**

belly day (cont'd)

MOVE 3: side planks
obliques

a. Lie on your left side with your legs extended and right arm resting against your right thigh. Prop up your upper body with your left forearm against the floor.

a

b. Exhale as you lift your hips off the floor as you simultaneously balance your body weight on your left forearm and outer edge of your left foot. Hold for 30 seconds, breathing normally. Switch sides and repeat, then move on to Move 4.

b

eat nutritionally, *not* emotionally®
visualization

For your visualizations for Level 2, you will use the power of your mind-body connection to fuel your motivation to complete your Cruise Moves and stick to your Cruise Down Plate and other healthy habits. During today's visualization, you will imagine a whole day's worth of your favorite

healthy food choices. So close your eyes and take a few deep, relaxing breaths, in through your nose and out through your mouth. Allow each exhalation to bring you to a state of deep relaxation. Once you feel completely relaxed, you're ready to begin.

MOVE 4: flat lifts
lower rectus abdominus

a. Lie on your back with your knees bent and feet flat on the floor. Rest your arms at your sides with your palms against the floor.

b. Exhale and tighten your abdomen as you lift and extend both legs, creating a 45-degree angle between your legs and the floor. Don't allow your lower back to arch away from the floor. Continue to breathe normally as you hold the move for 5 seconds. Lower your legs to the floor, rest for 2 seconds and then repeat. Alternate between repeating and resting for 1 minute, then return to Move 1 on page 102. Repeat Moves 1–4 once more, and you're done.

a

b

seeing healthy foods

You're heading to the kitchen to prepare a wholesome breakfast. Will you be filling your Cruise Down Plate with scrambled egg whites, whole-grain toast with a teaspoon of flax oil, and an orange?

Three hours later, it's time for a snack. Will you have a cup of yogurt? What about for lunch? Will you join a friend for sushi and soup? Three hours later, it's

time for another snack. What'll it be? Maybe a pudding cup? Three hours later, you've got a dinner date. Decide which veggies will fill your plate. What else will you have? And then you have a special treat, possibly a Hershey's Kiss. Imagine eating and enjoying each meal. Remember, your goal is to eat to create new lean muscles that burn that belly fat!

Level 2
Tuesday

"If you follow your bliss, doors will open up for you that wouldn't have opened for anyone else."

—Joseph Campbell

jorge's power thought

Water is so important to your success. Your body is made up of 75 percent water. Your body needs water to create a fluid blood volume. When you become dehydrated, your blood becomes viscous and sticky, making it harder for your heart to pump it through your body. This raises your heart rate, making you feel overly tired during simple movements like your Cruise Moves. Worse, your brain can't distinguish between dehydration and starvation, and responds to both by emitting hunger signals. This means that even though your body is not in need of food, you will feel fatigued, restless, and hungry, when all you really need is a tall glass of water.

"Every good thing you do for your body will help you reach your goal more quickly."

8 minute moves®
upper-body day

MOVE 1: table pump
chest

a. Sit on the edge of a sturdy chair 2 to 3 feet in front of a table. Place your palms on the tabletop with your arms extended. Don't lock your elbows; keep them soft. Sit tall with a long, straight back, relaxed shoulders, and firm abdominals.

b. Inhale as you bend your elbows and lean forward from your hips, bringing your chest toward the table. Once you can no longer bend forward, exhale as you press back to the starting position. Repeat for 1 minute, then move on to Move 2.

a

b

8-MINUTE LOG				
exercise	move 1	move 2	move 3	move 4
sets				
reps				

MOVE 2: roller-coaster pump
shoulders

a. Stand with your feet directly under your hips, your back long and straight, and your abs firm. Exhale as you raise your arms in front of your torso to shoulder level. Make sure to keep your shoulders relaxed away from your ears.

b. Lower your arms to the starting position as you inhale.

c. Exhale as you raise your arms out to your sides. Stop once they reach shoulder height, then inhale and lower them to the starting position. Repeat the entire sequence for 60 seconds, then move on to Move 3 on page 110.

a
b
c

exercise sequence

1. warm up Jog or march in place for 1 minute.

2. cruise moves Do one 60-second repetition of each of your 4 Cruise Moves. Repeat this cycle and you will be done in 8 minutes.

3. cool down After your Cruise Moves, do these stretches (see page 57).

Sky-reaching pose | Hurdler's stretch | Cobra stretch

upper-body day (cont'd)

MOVE 3: "show off my muscle" hold
biceps

a. Stand with your feet slightly wider than your hips. Firm your abdominals, lengthen and straighten your back, and relax your shoulders. Raise your arms out to the sides with your palms facing up. Curl your hands in loose fists toward your shoulders. Once in position, show off that muscle! Firm and flex your biceps and hold for 1 minute, then move on to Move 4.

a

eat nutritionally, *not* emotionally® visualization

It's a beautiful summer day, so today you will accompany a friend and her dog to the park for a day of sunshine and playing around. Get ready by closing your eyes and taking a few deep, relaxing breaths, in through your nose and out through your mouth. Allow each exhalation to bring you to a state of deep relaxation. Once you feel completely relaxed, you're ready to begin.

MOVE 4: kickback hold
triceps

a. Stand with your feet directly under your hips. Bend forward from your hips about 45 degrees with your arms extended toward the floor. Exhale as you lift your extended arms behind your torso, with your pinkies facing up. Stop once you've extended your arms, but before you've locked your elbows. (Remember: Never lock your joints. Always keep them soft.) Hold for 1 minute, then return to Move 1 on page 108. Repeat Moves 1–4 once more, and you're done.

a

a day at the park

Being active is a way of life for you. Feel the enjoyment from deep inside that comes from spending the day outdoors being active. You straighten your visor, grab a water bottle from the fridge, and step out your front door just as your friend and her dog are crossing the street.

The three of you walk the mile or so to the park, talking and laughing the whole way. As you enter the park, you stop off at a water fountain to refill your bottle and take a nice, long, refreshing sip. "Ahhh, that hits the spot!" you say. You head toward a big open lawn. Your buddy and you throw a Frisbee and chase her dog around the park. How great does it feel to be able to run and jump and play like a kid?

Level 2
Wednesday

"Do what you can,
with what you
have, where you
are."

—Theodore
Roosevelt

jorge's power thought

When your life becomes very busy, it's easy to slip off the exercise wagon and put your Cruise Moves at the bottom of your list of obligations. But don't! Not only are your Cruise Moves critical to your success, but they also will help you deal with the stress of general everyday life. When you exercise regularly, you're less likely to suffer from depression and the feeling of being overwhelmed. In turn, that makes you less likely to self-medicate with food. So, every morning—no matter if you're staying at a relative's home, sleeping in a hotel, or simply at home—perform your Cruise Moves as soon as you wake up. Then, throughout the day, perform mini exercise sessions. These can be as simple as a 5-minute stroll around the block or chasing your dog around the backyard. Any kind of movement you can squeeze in will leave you more energized, less stressed, and better able enjoy everything that life has to offer.

"Toss the memory of your unfit past into the trash. Walk into the world of fitness with confidence. Your possibilities are endless."

8 minute moves®
belly day

MOVE 1: vacuum on knees
transverse abdominus

a. Kneel on the floor in a table position with your hands under your shoulders and your knees under your hips. Make sure your spine remains in a neutral position.

b. Exhale as you bring your belly button in toward your spine and contract your abdominal muscles. Bring your belly as far inward as it will go. Hold for 1 to 3 seconds, then exhale and expand your belly as much as it will expand. Continue alternating slowly between the two positions for 1 minute, then move on to Move 2.

a

b

8-MINUTE LOG				
exercise	move 1	move 2	move 3	move 4
sets				
reps				

MOVE 2: plank
rectus abdomimus

a. Lie on your belly with your legs extended. Bend your arms and place your forearms against the floor with your elbows under your shoulders.

a

b. Exhale as you lift your torso into a modified push-up position. Only the balls of your feet and your hands and forearms should touch the floor. Try to form a straight line from your heels to your head, using the strength of your belly to prevent your hips from sagging down toward the floor. Breathe normally as you hold this move. Eventually you want to hold this move for 1 minute, but at first you may only be able to manage 10 seconds. Hold for as long as you can, then move on to Move 3 on page 116.

b

exercise sequence

1. warm up Jog or march in place for 1 minute.

2. cruise moves Do one 60-second repetition of each of your 4 Cruise Moves. Repeat this cycle and you will be done in 8 minutes.

3. cool down After your Cruise Moves, do these stretches (see page 57).

Sky-reaching pose | **Hurdler's stretch** | **Cobra stretch**

belly day (cont'd)

MOVE 3: side planks
obliques

a. Lie on your left side with your legs extended and right arm resting against your right thigh. Prop up your upper body with your left forearm against the floor.

b. Exhale as you lift your hips off the floor as you simultaneously balance your body weight on your left forearm and outer edge of your left foot. Hold for 30 seconds, breathing normally. Switch sides and repeat, then move on to Move 4.

a

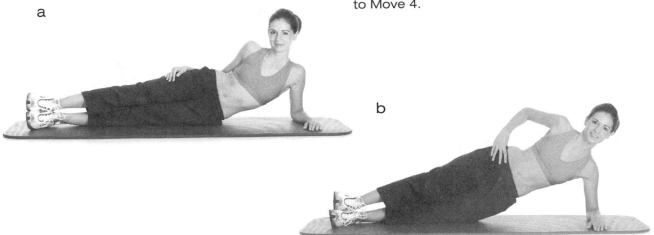

b

eat nutritionally, *not* emotionally®
visualization

Your commitment to living a healthy lifestyle has changed every aspect of your life for the better, and not only are you happier than you've ever been, but your body is becoming toned, tight, strong, and lean. Today you're going to be showing it off as you participate in a health and fitness contest! So close your eyes and take a few relaxing breaths, in through your nose and out through your mouth. Allow each exhalation to bring you to a state of deep relaxation. Once you feel completely relaxed, you're ready to begin.

MOVE 4: flat lifts
lower rectus abdominus

a. Lie on your back with your knees bent and feet flat on the floor. Rest your arms at your sides with your palms against the floor.

a

b. Exhale and tighten your abdomen as you lift and extend both legs, creating a 45-degree angle between your legs and the floor. Don't allow your lower back to arch away from the floor. Continue to breathe normally as you hold the move for 5 seconds. Lower your legs to the floor, rest for 2 seconds and then repeat. Alternate between repeating and resting for 1 minute, then return to Move 1 on page 114. Repeat Moves 1–4 once more, and you're done.

b

the fittest person of the year

You've just arrived at the auditorium where you'll be competing for the title of "Healthiest and Fittest Person of the Year." A stage manager escorts you to your dressing room, which is filled with flowers and cards from friends and family.

You change into your outfit and do some stretches. When it is your turn, you confidently jog onto the stage. The music starts and you flawlessly perform your moves. How does your body feel as it twists, bends, and jumps? You hit the mark on your final move and hold it for a few seconds as the crowd goes wild. "Ladies and gentlemen," the announcer says, "You are looking at your new Healthiest and Fittest Person of the Year!" How great do you feel?

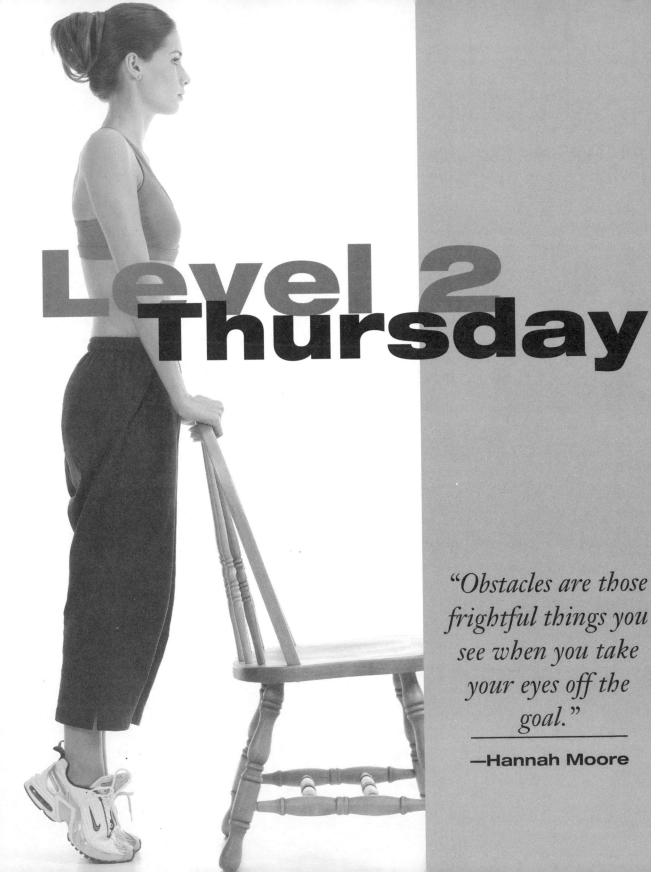

Level 2
Thursday

"Obstacles are those frightful things you see when you take your eyes off the goal."

—Hannah Moore

jorge's power thought

Many of the foods that we so endearingly refer to as comfort foods—like chicken pot pie, chili, mashed potatoes, and macaroni and cheese—are loaded with saturated fat. That means they settle a bit too comfortably on your waist! But comfort foods don't have to be loaded with fat and calories to give you that warm, cozy feeling. Warm foods with a high water or fiber content can fit the bill and are especially satisfying. A cup of vegetable soup or oatmeal is a great, healthy choice. Or if you'd like something creamy, you can create that texture using pureed white beans, silken tofu, or instant low-calorie potato flakes. For a healthier chili, substitute ground turkey for the beef, and top it with reduced-fat cheese. Remember, with a little creativity, you can make any food into a healthful food.

"There are so many places your body can take you. The stronger you become, the more you can experience. There is nothing beyond your grasp."

8 minute moves®
lower-body day

MOVE 1: superman
lower back

a. Lie with your belly on the floor, your legs straight, and your arms extended in front of you, like Superman flying through the air. Exhale as you simultaneously lift your arms and legs about 4 inches off the floor. If you begin to feel pinching in your lower back, focus on lengthening your spine by reaching out through your fingertips and toes. Make sure your head remains in a neutral position with your gaze straight ahead. Hold for 1 minute, then move on to Move 2.

a

8-MINUTE LOG				
exercise	move 1	move 2	move 3	move 4
sets				
reps				

MOVE 2: wall hold
quadriceps

a. Stand with your feet directly under your hips and your head, shoulders, and back against a wall. Slowly walk your feet forward as you bend your knees, sliding downward along the wall as far as you can without bringing your knees past your ankles or your buttocks below your knees. Hold for 1 minute as you breathe normally, then move on to Move 3 on page 122.

a

exercise sequence

1. warm up Jog or march in place for 1 minute.

2. cruise moves Do one 60-second repetition of each of your 4 Cruise Moves. Repeat this cycle and you will be done in 8 minutes.

3. cool down After your Cruise Moves, do these stretches (see page 57).

Sky-reaching pose | **Hurdler's stretch** | **Cobra stretch**

lower-body day (cont'd)

MOVE 3: hamstring lift hold
hamstrings

a. Stand about 1 foot in front of a wall with your feet directly under your hips. Rest your hands against the wall for balance. Check your posture. Make sure your back is long and straight, your abs are firm, and your shoulders are relaxed away from your ears.

b. Exhale as you lift your right foot toward your right buttock. Stop once you achieve a 90-degree angle. Hold for 30 seconds as you breathe normally, then switch legs. Once you've repeated with the other leg, move on to Move 4.

a

b

eat nutritionally, *not* emotionally®
visualization

Today you're going to prepare a delicious salad made with vegetables you've grown yourself in your very own garden. Today's visualization will make it possible! Close your eyes and take a few relaxing breaths, in through your nose and out through your mouth. Allow each exhalation to bring you to a state of deep relaxation. Once you feel completely relaxed, you're ready to begin.

MOVE 4: high heel hold
calves

a. Stand with your feet directly under your hips. Exhale as you lift your heels, rising onto the balls of your feet. Place one hand on a sturdy chair or wall for balance. Pretend you are wearing very high heels. Hold for 1 minute, then return to Move 1 on page 120. Repeat Moves 1–4 once more, and you're done.

a

your inner garden

You've just returned home from your local garden center with everything you need to start your garden—soil, seeds, transplants, shovel, hoe, watering can, and gloves. You slip on a pair of overalls, rub on some sunscreen, and place a wide-brimmed hat on your head.

Feel the sun warm your cheeks as you start hoeing the soil. Your arms are strong and firm. As you dig the soil and plant each seed or transplant, concentrate on how strong your body feels. You treat the garden with gentle care, giving it the nutrients it needs to grow! Picture how the garden will look in a few weeks and then in a month. Imagine the vegetables growing ripe and delicious.

Level 2
Friday

"Make it a rule of
life to never regret
and never look
back. Regret is
an appalling waste
of energy."

—Katherine
Mansfield

jorge's power thought

When you add flax oil to your meal (or take it in capsule form), it will become one of the key building materials in creating your new lean muscle, plus it will help to suppress your appetite, unlock and burn stored body fat, and improve your overall health. It can do all of these amazing things because it is the richest source of omega-3 fats. These fats are your body's top choice for maintaining everything from cell membranes to brain function. And when your body uses omega-3 fats for these types of necessary bodily functions, there is literally no more of it left to be stored on your body as fat. I suggest buying the oil and mixing a teaspoon of it into oatmeal, yogurt, and other foods. You won't notice the taste once you mix it in, but later, you'll notice how full you feel! For more information on flaxseed oil and my top brand pick, visit www.jorgecruise.com.

"Relish every compliment you receive about your belly. Let each compliment fuel your motivation for more."

8 minute moves®
belly day

MOVE 1: vacuum on knees
transverse abdominus

a. Kneel on the floor in a table position with your hands under your shoulders and your knees under your hips. Make sure your spine remains in a neutral position.

b. Exhale as you bring your belly button in toward your spine and contract your abdominal muscles. Bring your belly as far inward as it will go. Hold for 1 to 3 seconds, then exhale and expand your belly as much as it will expand. Continue alternating slowly between the two positions for 1 minute, then move on to Move 2.

a

b

8-MINUTE LOG				
exercise	move 1	move 2	move 3	move 4
sets				
reps				

MOVE 2: plank
rectus abdomimus

a. Lie on your belly with your legs extended. Bend your arms and place your forearms against the floor with your elbows under your shoulders.

a

b. Exhale as you lift your torso into a modified push-up position. Only the balls of your feet and your hands and forearms should touch the floor. Try to form a straight line from your heels to your head, using the strength of your belly to prevent your hips from sagging down toward the floor. Breathe normally as you hold this move. Eventually you want to hold this move for 1 minute, but at first you may only be able to manage 10 seconds. Hold for as long as you can, then move on to Move 3 on page 128.

b

exercise sequence

1. warm up Jog or march in place for 1 minute.

2. cruise moves Do one 60-second repetition of each of your 4 Cruise Moves. Repeat this cycle and you will be done in 8 minutes.

3. cool down After your Cruise Moves, do these stretches (see page 57).

Sky-reaching pose | **Hurdler's stretch** | **Cobra stretch**

belly day (cont'd)

MOVE 3: side planks
obliques

a. Lie on your left side with your legs extended and right arm resting against your right thigh. Prop up your upper body with your left forearm against the floor.

b. Exhale as you lift your hips off the floor as you simultaneously balance your body weight on your left forearm and outer edge of your left foot. Hold for 30 seconds, breathing normally. Switch sides and repeat, then move on to Move 4.

a

b

eat nutritionally, *not* emotionally®
visualization

For today's visualization exercise, you're going to feel the breeze run through your hair as you and a friend take a leisurely bike ride through your neighborhood. Get ready to hop on for a fun-filled ride! Close your eyes and take a few relaxing breaths, in through your nose and out through your mouth. Allow each exhalation to bring you to a state of deep relaxation. Once you feel completely relaxed, you're ready to begin.

MOVE 4: flat lifts
lower rectus abdominus

a. Lie on your back with your knees bent and feet flat on the floor. Rest your arms at your sides with your palms against the floor.

a

b. Exhale and tighten your abdomen as you lift and extend both legs, creating a 45-degree angle between your legs and the floor. Don't allow your lower back to arch away from the floor. Continue to breathe normally as you hold the move for 5 seconds. Lower your legs to the floor, rest for 2 seconds and then repeat. Alternate between repeating and resting for 1 minute, then return to Move 1 on page 126. Repeat Moves 1–4 once more, and you're done.

b

a fit you

Picture yourself dressed in a pair of comfortable spandex shorts and a nice, cool T-shirt. You're doing a few stretches as you wait for your friend to arrive.

"You all set?" your friend asks as she steers her bike into your driveway. "Yep," you reply, "Let me just go get my bike."

You wheel your bike around the side of your house and think about how fun it is to be able to enjoy a day of bike riding. You and your friend pedal along, talking and laughing. Sometimes you ride slowly and leisurely, and other times you pick up the pace and playfully race one another. You feel like a kid again as you glide through your neighborhood, enjoying the scenery and the sun on your face.

Level 2
Saturday

"Character is
what you are in
the dark."

—Dwight L. Moody

jorge's power thought

Most people need at least 8 hours of sleep a night in order to fully rest, repair, and rejuvenate their bodies. If you've gotten into the habit of staying up late and not giving your body as much sleep as it needs, start taking baby steps toward getting to bed earlier. Since your body has an internal clock that is set according to your routine habits, you'll probably have a hard time falling asleep an hour or more earlier than you're used to. So change your bedtime in 15-minute increments so your body's clock will be able to appropriately readjust. Also, the more dependent you are on caffeine, the harder it will be for you to wake up in the morning. Wean yourself off excessive caffeine by switching to half-caffeine and half-decaf coffee. From there switch to either tea or all-decaf coffee. From there switch to green tea or decaffeinated tea.

"As you cleanse today, mentally allow yourself to release some negativity from your past. Notice the freedom you feel simply by adopting a positive outlook."

body cleanse
day off from cruise moves

Today is your day off from Cruise Moves, but not a day off from the program. Use today to pamper yourself inside and out. Spend some time relaxing—both your mind and body. Read that novel that you've been putting off. Spend some time at the park, writing in the journal provided on the following page. Or take a nap in the afternoon! This is your day to rest, relax, and rejuvenate, your day to completely cleanse your body.

To cleanse your body, follow my three-step plan:

1. Drink your psyllium shake for breakfast. The shake replaces your meal. Don't have anything for breakfast other than your shake. (To purchase psyllium husk powder, visit www.jorgecruise.com.)

2. Make both lunch and dinner's protein serving non-meat options. See the bonus chapter on page 319 for sample vegetable protein meals.

3. Drink eight 16-ounce glasses of water, doubling your usual water intake.

eat nutritionally, *not* emotionally®
visualization

Today is your good friend's birthday and you've invited her over for a healthy and delicious gourmet dinner. Are you ready to get cooking? Close your eyes and take a few relaxing breaths, in through your nose and out through your mouth. Allow each exhalation to bring you to a state of deep relaxation. Once you feel completely relaxed, you're ready to begin.

journal _____ _____
_____ _____
_____ _____
_____ _____
_____ _____
_____ _____
_____ _____
_____ _____
_____ _____
_____ _____
_____ _____
_____ _____
_____ _____
_____ _____
_____ _____
_____ _____
_____ _____
_____ _____
_____ _____

a gourmet meal

You carefully planned the menu earlier in the week and purchased everything you need.

You hear the doorbell ring just as you finish chopping the last few veggies for the salad. See yourself opening the door and greeting your friend with a big birthday hug. As she follows you into the kitchen, she comments on how delicious everything smells. You lead her to the dining table, which you've set with your best dishes and decorated with a vase full of her favorite flowers. See yourself serving each yummy dish as the birthday girl "oohs" and "ahhs." Enjoy each bite and stop eating when you're satisfied, not overly full.

When dinner is cleared, you dim the lights and bring out the cake. She blows out the candles and you each savor a delectable slice. As she prepares to leave, you box up the leftovers for her to enjoy the next day. She gives you a big hug and says, "Thank you so much! This really made me feel special. You are a great friend."

Level 2
Sunday

"Most people spend their lives struggling with the same old road, wondering whether they will ever reach their

dreams. The lucky ones discover there's a beautiful six-lane expressway just over the hill, created just for them. It's their personal path, ready and waiting to speed them to their dreams."

—Chris J. Witting Jr.

jorge's power thought

Chromium picolinate is a mineral that your body needs to build muscle and reduce body fat. You need only a very small amount, but a startling 50 percent of Americans probably don't consume enough of this important mineral to do the job. Chromium simply is not readily available in that many healthful foods. That's why I recommend that you take a chromium supplement. Your minimum daily dosage should be 200 micrograms, but for even better results, shoot for 400 to 600 micrograms a day. You won't see results right away; it usually takes about 6 months before your body adjusts to the extra dose of this mineral. However, rest assured that you eventually will notice a positive change. After taking chromium supplements for a few months, my clients reported fewer food cravings and more endurance during their Cruise Moves.

"Whenever you find yourself struggling with temptation, remember your Seatbelts. That's what they're for!"

capture your progress
day off from cruise moves

Today is your day off. Take a moment to relish your progress. Grab a pen and answer the following questions. Then share the answers with me by sending an e-mail to flatbelly2@jorgecruise.com.

1. What is your current weight?

_____

2. What was your original weight?

_____

3. What is your waist circumference in inches?

_____

4. What was your original waist circumference in inches?

_____

5. What have you done well this week? What are you most proud of?

_____

_____

_____

_____

_____

6. What could you improve next week?

_____

_____

_____

_____

_____

eat nutritionally, *not* emotionally®
visualization

For today's visualization we are going to take a look at a typical morning in your future life. You've got errands to run, jobs to do, people to see, and traffic to sit in—hey, that's life! But the morning—that's *your* time. Close your eyes and take a few relaxing breaths, in through your nose and out through your mouth. Allow each exhalation to bring you to a state of deep relaxation. Once you feel completely relaxed, you're ready to begin.

edna frizzell shrank four dress sizes!

"I started the program 8 months after giving birth to my second child in order to lose the weight I had gained during my pregnancy. The Cruise Moves helped to give me the slender, firmer look I had been craving for such a long time. I can now wear more stylish clothes and feel comfortable in a bathing suit. Best of all, the program also fit into my busy schedule. I was able to see results quickly, and that gave me the motivation to keep going.

"Besides shrinking the size of my belly, I also experienced other results. I now have my self-esteem back, which is one of the best benefits of the program. I love who I am and I can actually look in the mirror and like who I see. My bubbly personality is back. I feel young again and I look great! Thank you, Jorge, for bringing me back!"

Edna lost 25 pounds!

morning insight

See yourself in your bed just before you are about to wake up. Look at how peaceful and rested you are, how easy your breathing is. Watch as you wake up and look at the clock. You don't even need an alarm clock anymore because your internal clock wakes you up naturally right at 6:00 A.M. every morning. Watch as you stretch your toned, strong arm over to your bedside table and pull a card from a stack of motivational messages that you've made for yourself. Once you read it, you jump out of bed and head for the bathroom to freshen up. Once out, you tackle your Cruise Moves.

Look at your muscles contract as you perform each controlled, smooth rep. Did you ever imagine your belly could look like this? After 8 minutes you wrap up with some cooldown stretches. You love having that time all for yourself in the morning. Now, you hit the shower and get dressed for your day. Look at yourself in the mirror and smile. It's going to be a great day!

Level 3
Monday

jorge's power thought

Brown rice is an excellent addition to any meal. It has a rich, chewy texture that is great as a side dish; mixed with beans, herbs, vegetables, or chicken; or added to a burrito or soup. A serving of brown rice is a great source of selenium, which can cut your cancer and heart disease risk. And it also contains 2 milligrams of vitamin E, which is an excellent antioxidant that helps repair your muscles after your Cruise Moves.

In addition to brown rice, I also love to eat oats. I love to add oats to homemade chicken soup. Oats are packed with soluble fiber (the type that lowers cholesterol and aids digestion), copper, magnesium, and zinc. If you eat oatmeal, make sure to buy the slow-cooking variety. Instant oatmeal is much more refined and has less fiber than slower-cooking oats.

"Give yourself a gift: Forgive someone today. Notice how much energy is created when you release your grip on anger."

8 minute moves®
belly day

MOVE 1: vacuum with swiss ball
transverse abdominus

a. Stand while holding a large, air-filled fitness ball (also called a Swiss ball) against your belly with both hands. Completely exhale as you bring your belly button in toward your spine. Hold for 1 to 3 seconds. Then, as you inhale, try to expand your belly into the ball—pushing the ball away—as you simultaneously use your hands to hold the ball in position, creating resistance against your belly. Once you've completely inhaled, hold for 1 to 3 seconds. Alternate between the two positions for 1 minute, then move on to Move 2.

a

8-MINUTE LOG				
exercise	move 1	move 2	move 3	move 4
sets				
reps				

MOVE 2: jackknife with swiss ball
rectus abdominus

a. Stand with your fitness ball in front of you. Kneel into the ball and walk your hands forward until you can place one palm and then the other onto the floor in front of your ball, with your shins on the ball. Continue to slowly walk your hands forward on the floor, until you are in a push-up position with your shins on the ball and your hands under your chest.

b. Tighten your abs to keep your hips from sagging toward the floor. Exhale as you bend your knees, bringing your thighs into your chest as you simultaneously roll the ball forward. Hold for 1 to 3 seconds, then inhale as you return to the starting position. Alternate between the two positions for 1 minute, then move on to Move 3 on page 142.

a

b

exercise sequence

1. warm up Jog or march in place for 1 minute.

2. cruise moves Do one 60-second repetition of each of your 4 Cruise Moves. Repeat this cycle and you will be done in 8 minutes.

3. cool down After your Cruise Moves, do these stretches (see page 57).

Sky-reaching pose | **Hurdler's stretch** | **Cobra stretch**

belly day (cont'd)

MOVE 3: leg rolls with swiss ball
obliques

a. Lie on your back with your arms out to the sides and your palms against the floor. Grasp a fitness ball between your ankles with your legs extended toward the ceiling.

b. Exhale as you slowly lower your legs to the right. Try to keep both shoulder blades against the floor as you twist. Inhale as you return to the starting position, then exhale as you drop your legs to the left. Continue alternating between right and left for 1 minute, then move on to Move 4.

a

b

eat nutritionally, *not emotionally*® visualization

During your Level 3 visualizations, you will use the power of your mind-body connection to help solve the emotional problems and stress that may lead to overeating or under-exercising. For today's visualization, I'd like you to explore your own passion and see where it will take you. Close your eyes and take a few deep, relaxing breaths, in through your nose and out through your mouth. Allow each exhalation to bring you to a state of deep relaxation. Once you feel completely relaxed, you're ready to begin.

MOVE 4: v-sit with swiss ball
lower rectus abdominus

a. Sit on the floor with your legs extended. Hold a fitness ball between your palms with your arms extended at chest level.

b. Exhale as you lean back slightly and lift your legs until you form a V-shape with your torso. Hold for up to 1 minute, then return to Move 1 on page 140. Repeat Moves 1–4 once more, and you're done.

a

b

unleash your inner passion

Visualize yourself 1 year in the future. See yourself as you would like to be. You are accomplishing all of the things that you wanted with strength and vigor. You are focusing on what's most important to you and making your mark on the world.

What does this new world look like? What new mental, physical, and spiritual qualities have you uncovered? What accomplishments are you most proud of? What was most important in helping you to achieve success? What helped you to overcome any challenges along the way?

With those answers, take a step back to the present moment and visualize what you must do right now to make your future become reality.

Level 3
Tuesday

"The first step towards getting somewhere is deciding that you are not going to stay where you are."

—J. Pierpont Morgan

jorge's power thought

Even if you eat a healthful diet that is rich in vegetables and whole grains, you may still be deficient in many important nutrients. In fact, the *Journal of the American Medical Association* has recently reported that "most people do not consume an optimal amount of all vitamins by diet alone," and that "all adults should take one multivitamin daily." Taking a multivitamin provides extra insurance that you get all of the vitamins and minerals you need, particularly on those extra-busy days when you don't eat as well as you should.

"Keep your eye on your goal. How great will you feel when you have a beautiful belly? How incredible will your life become?"

8 minute moves®
upper-body day

MOVE 1: push-ups on fitness ball
chest

a. Kneel on your fitness ball and place your palms on the floor in front of the ball. Walk your hands forward as you slide your legs forward along the ball, until the ball rests under your shins and your body is in a push-up position with your hands under your chest.

b. Inhale as you bend your elbows and lower your chest to the floor. Make sure to keep your abdomen strong and your back straight. Don't allow your hips to sag downward. Once your elbows bend 90 degrees, exhale as you push yourself back to the starting position. Repeat for 1 minute, then move on to Move 2.

a

b

8-MINUTE LOG				
exercise	move 1	move 2	move 3	move 4
sets				
reps				

MOVE 2: front raise with heavy ball
shoulders

a. Sit on your fitness ball with your knees bent and your feet on the floor. Grasp a heavy ball in both hands with your arms extended near your knees. Your hands should be on either side of the ball.

b. Exhale as you raise the ball to shoulder height. Inhale as you lower it to the starting position. Repeat for 1 minute, then move on to Move 3 on page 148.

a

b

exercise sequence

1. warm up Jog or march in place for 1 minute.

2. cruise moves Do one 60-second repetition of each of your 4 Cruise Moves. Repeat this cycle and you will be done in 8 minutes.

3. cool down After your Cruise Moves, do these stretches (see page 57).

Sky-reaching pose | **Hurdler's stretch** | **Cobra stretch**

upper-body day (cont'd)

MOVE 3: curls with heavy ball
biceps

a. Sit on your fitness ball with your knees bent and your feet on the floor. Grasp a heavy ball in both hands with your arms extended and your palms facing up.

b. Exhale as you bend your arms, curling the ball in toward your chest. Inhale as you lower the ball to the starting position. Repeat for 1 minute, then move on to Move 4.

a

b

eat nutritionally, *not* emotionally® visualization

Visualization can help you to face life's little challenges with more ease. Instead of problems, you see solutions. When life throws you a lemon, you can easily turn it into lemonade! Let's use visualization to help you turn your first lemon into *lemonaid*, shall we? Close your eyes and take a few deep, relaxing breaths, in through your nose and out through your mouth. Allow each exhalation to bring you to a state of deep relaxation. Once you feel completely relaxed, you're ready to begin.

MOVE 4: heavy ball drop
triceps

a. Sit on your fitness ball with your knees bent and your feet on the floor. Grasp your heavy ball in both hands and extend your arms overhead, with your upper arms close to your ears.

b. Inhale as you slowly bend your elbows and lower the ball behind your head. When you can lower the ball no further, exhale as you raise the ball back to the starting position. Repeat for 1 minute, then return to Move 1 on page 146. Repeat Moves 1–4 once more, and you're done.

a

b

mental lemonade

See yourself driving home happily singing along to the radio. Suddenly, you hear a "clunk, clunk, clunk" sound as your car begins to bounce around. It's a flat tire! You calmly steer your car to the side of the road and turn on your hazard lights. Carefully you open your door and assess the situation, then you go to your trunk and retrieve the spare tire, car jack, and lug wrench. See yourself quickly and easily replace the flat tire with the spare. Doesn't it feel great to have such strong arms? Once you replace the hubcap, you're on your way. No problem! How do you feel knowing that you can overcome any obstacle that comes up?

Level 3
Wednesday

"Attitude is greatly shaped by influence and association."

—Jim Rohn

jorge's power thought

After you complete your Cruise Moves in the morning, it is important to cool down with a quick full-body stretching routine. Stretching out your muscles after you train them helps to neutralize the effects of lactic acid by restoring bloodflow. Lactic acid is responsible for the burning sensation that you feel during your last few reps, making it harder to do another. Stretching helps to flush this byproduct from your body and regenerates your muscle capacity. Stretching also expedites the delivery of nutrients to your muscles, which accelerates the healing process. This means that you will diminish the amount of muscle soreness and post-workout fatigue. And most important, stretching will allow you to better recuperate between workouts, allowing you to come back stronger for your next Cruise Moves session (see page 57).

"What have you learned since you've started the program? I bet once you take a moment to think about it, you'll find that you've learned a great deal!"

8 minute moves®
belly day

MOVE 1: vacuum with swiss ball
transverse abdominus

a. Stand while holding a large, air-filled fitness ball (also called a Swiss ball) against your belly with both hands. Completely exhale as you bring your belly button in toward your spine. Hold for 1 to 3 seconds. Then, as you inhale, try to expand your belly into the ball—pushing the ball away—as you simultaneously use your hands to hold the ball in position, creating resistance against your belly. Once you've completely inhaled, hold for 1 to 3 seconds. Alternate between the two positions for 1 minute, then move on to Move 2.

a

8-MINUTE LOG				
exercise	move 1	move 2	move 3	move 4
sets				
reps				

MOVE 2: jackknife with swiss ball
rectus abdominus

a. Stand with your fitness ball in front of you. Kneel into the ball and walk your hands forward until you can place one palm and then the other onto the floor in front of your ball, with your shins on the ball. Continue to slowly walk your hands forward on the floor, until you are in a push-up position with your shins on the ball and your hands under your chest.

b. Tighten your abs to keep your hips from sagging toward the floor. Exhale as you bend your knees, bringing your thighs into your chest as you simultaneously roll the ball forward. Hold for 1 to 3 seconds, then inhale as you return to the starting position. Alternate between the two positions for 1 minute, then move on to Move 3 on page 154.

a

b

exercise sequence

1. warm up Jog or march in place for 1 minute.

2. cruise moves Do one 60-second repetition of each of your 4 Cruise Moves. Repeat this cycle and you will be done in 8 minutes.

3. cool down After your Cruise Moves, do these stretches (see page 57).

Sky-reaching pose | **Hurdler's stretch** | **Cobra stretch**

belly day (cont'd)

MOVE 3: leg rolls with swiss ball
obliques

a. Lie on your back with your arms out to the sides and your palms against the floor. Grasp a fitness ball between your ankles with your legs extended toward the ceiling.

b. Exhale as you slowly lower your legs to the right. Try to keep both shoulder blades against the floor as you twist. Inhale as you return to the starting position, then exhale as you drop your legs to the left. Continue alternating between right and left for 1 minute, then move on to Move 4.

a

b

eat nutritionally, *not* emotionally®
visualization

Many people think that the opposite of love is hate. It's not. The opposite of love is apathy. Love and hate, in fact, are very closely connected. All too often, it's the people we love the most that tend to make us the angriest. But you can use visualization to your advantage. Close your eyes and take a few deep, relaxing breaths, in through your nose and out through your mouth. Allow each exhalation to bring you to a state of deep relaxation. Once you feel completely relaxed, you're ready to begin.

MOVE 4: v-sit with swiss ball
lower rectus abdominus

a. Sit on the floor with your legs extended. Hold a fitness ball between your palms with your arms extended at chest level.

b. Exhale as you lean back slightly and lift your legs until you form a V-shape with your torso. Hold for up to 1 minute, then return to Move 1 on page 152. Repeat Moves 1–4 once more, and you're done.

a

b

seeing your problems vanish

I want you to imagine someone with whom you are having a personal conflict. It might be your spouse or your child or someone at work. Bring the image of that person into your mind. Then imagine having a positive interaction with that person. Start with some small talk. Then see yourself confronting this person about what is bothering you. See yourself calmly, nicely, and succinctly voicing your concerns, focusing on how this person makes you feel. See this person respond positively, perhaps by saying, "I didn't know you felt this way." You will soon find that if you mentally see yourself confronting your problems, you won't feel so much stress or anxiety when you try to solve them in real life!

Level 3
Thursday

"It takes 17 muscles to smile and 47 muscles to frown. Conserve energy."

—Unknown

jorge's power thought

Eggs have gotten a bad rap over the last few decades because health experts thought that eggs raised blood cholesterol levels. In the last few years, however, numerous health organizations have been vindicating eggs' reputation. Although egg yolks are high in cholesterol, they don't seem to raise blood cholesterol in most people. That's good news because eggs provide a great source of the quality protein that your muscles need in order to grow. They also contain vitamin E, which helps protect muscle cells from oxidation, as well as a number of important B vitamins that help your body burn fat. Most of the saturated fat in an egg is in the yolk, so I suggest you just eat the protein-rich egg white or try an egg substitute product, like Egg Beaters.

"How have you changed since you started the program? By now your body has probably changed quite a bit. How about your mind and your emotions?"

8 minute moves®
lower-body day

MOVE 1: extensions on ball
lower back

a. Lie with your belly on your fitness ball. Place your toes on the floor as wide apart as you need in order to keep your balance. Place your fingers behind your head with your elbows out to the sides. Your body should form a straight line from your heels to your head.

b. Inhale as you lower your torso toward the ball. Once your chest reaches the ball, exhale as you rise to the starting position. Repeat for 1 minute, then move on to Move 2.

a

b

8-MINUTE LOG				
exercise	move 1	move 2	move 3	move 4
sets				
reps				

MOVE 2: ball squats
quadriceps

a. Place your fitness ball between your back and a wall, leaning your body weight into the ball to hold it in place. Place your feet 1 to 2 feet away from the wall, hip-width apart.

b. Inhale as you bend your knees to 90 degrees, making sure your knees remain above your ankles. If they jut out farther than your arches or toes, move your feet a few more inches away from the wall. Exhale as you straighten your legs, rolling the ball up the wall as you do so. Continue to alternate between the two positions for 1 minute, then move on to Move 3 on page 160.

a

b

exercise sequence

1. warm up Jog or march in place for 1 minute.

2. cruise moves Do one 60-second repetition of each of your 4 Cruise Moves. Repeat this cycle and you will be done in 8 minutes.

3. cool down After your Cruise Moves, do these stretches (see page 57).

Sky-reaching pose | **Hurdler's stretch** | **Cobra stretch**

lower-body day (cont'd)

MOVE 3: walking lunges with ball
hamstrings

a. Stand with your feet under your hips. Grasp your fitness ball between your hands, holding it at chest height. Inhale as you take a large step forward with your right leg and bend both knees into 90-degree angles. At the same time, twist your torso to the right, keeping your back upright. Exhale as you take another step forward, this time lunging forward with your left leg and twisting your torso to the left. Continue to lunge forward for 1 minute, then move on to Move 4.

a

eat nutritionally, *not* emotionally® visualization

I've told you that your first step to eliminating emotional eating begins with you. It begins with treating yourself with the utmost respect, and you can do that only if you love yourself and your body. Sometimes cultivating self-love in the place of self-hate can be difficult. Today, you will complete a visualization that will help. Close your eyes and take a few deep, relaxing breaths, in through your nose and out through your mouth. Allow each exhalation to bring you to a state of deep relaxation. Once you feel completely relaxed, you're ready to begin.

MOVE 4: calf raises with ball
calves

a. Stand with your left leg bent and the top of your left foot on top of your fitness ball. Adjust your body weight so that you feel firmly balanced. Stand tall with good posture.

b. Exhale as you raise your right heel off the floor, bringing your body weight onto the ball of your right foot. Inhale as you lower. Continue your calf raises for 30 seconds and then switch sides. Do calf raises on your left foot for 30 seconds, then return to Move 1 on page 158. Repeat Moves 1–4 once more, and you're done.

a

b

cultivating inner love

Think back to a time in your life when you felt good about yourself. Perhaps you accomplished something significant, won an award, or got a promotion at work. Whatever it was, bring the memory of that happy time fully into your awareness.

See every detail of that moment. Try to feel the emotions that you felt during that happy time.

Think back to the smells, sights, sounds, and sensations of that moment. Try to recall it as vividly as possible. Take a few moments to relish the good feeling that you've just created inside of yourself. Know that these positive feelings are always there inside of you, waiting to be called upon at any moment.

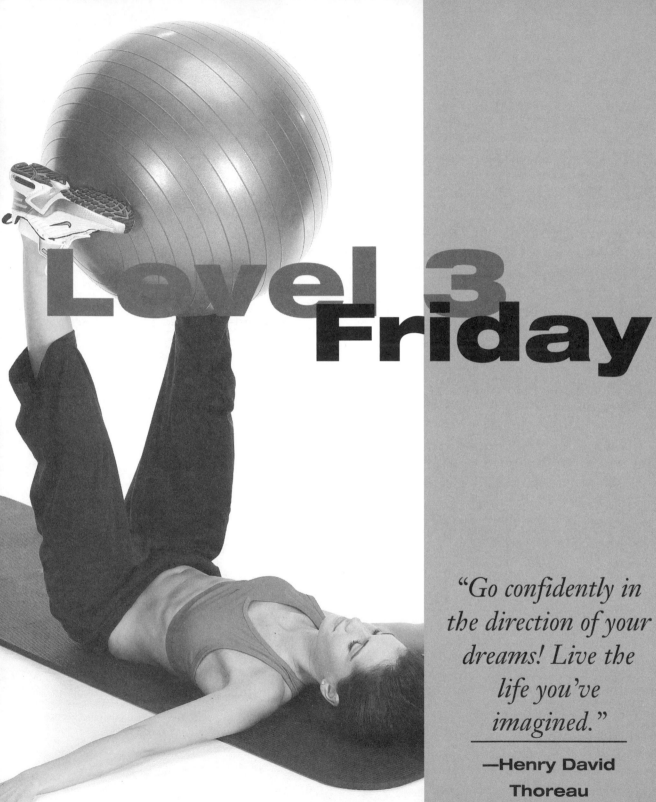

Level 3
Friday

"*Go confidently in the direction of your dreams! Live the life you've imagined.*"

—**Henry David Thoreau**

jorge's power thought

Lean beef and skinless poultry provide excellent low-fat sources of protein and can make for delicious meals—if you know how to cook them. Many people get frustrated when they cook lean protein sources because they think it tastes dry and tough. You can reclaim the tenderness of lean protein foods by cooking them at low temperatures. Lean meats—chicken breast, pork tenderloin, or lean cuts of beef—cook best with a slow-cooking method, like braising or stewing. You'll get better flavor if you brown or sear the meat first. This will help to lock in the moisture. Then, add liquid, such as broth, wine, or juice and cook at a simmer.

"You've come so far. Reward yourself. Buy a new outfit, spend a day at a spa, or buy tickets to a show or concert. You deserve it!"

8 minute moves®
belly day

MOVE 1: vacuum with swiss ball
transverse abdominus

a. Stand while holding a large, air-filled fitness ball (also called a Swiss ball) against your belly with both hands. Completely exhale as you bring your belly button in toward your spine. Hold for 1 to 3 seconds. Then, as you inhale, try to expand your belly into the ball—pushing the ball away—as you simultaneously use your hands to hold the ball in position, creating resistance against your belly. Once you've completely inhaled, hold for 1 to 3 seconds. Alternate between the two positions for 1 minute, then move on to Move 2.

a

8-MINUTE LOG				
exercise	move 1	move 2	move 3	move 4
sets				
reps				

MOVE 2: jackknife with swiss ball
rectus abdominus

a. Stand with your fitness ball in front of you. Kneel into the ball and walk your hands forward until you can place one palm and then the other onto the floor in front of your ball, with your shins on the ball. Continue to slowly walk your hands forward on the floor, until you are in a push-up position with your shins on the ball and your hands under your chest.

b. Tighten your abs to keep your hips from sagging toward the floor. Exhale as you bend your knees, bringing your thighs into your chest as you simultaneously roll the ball forward. Hold for 1 to 3 seconds, then inhale as you return to the starting position. Alternate between the two positions for 1 minute, then move on to Move 3 on page 166.

a

b

exercise sequence

1. warm up Jog or march in place for 1 minute.

2. cruise moves Do one 60-second repetition of each of your 4 Cruise Moves. Repeat this cycle and you will be done in 8 minutes.

3. cool down After your Cruise Moves, do these stretches (see page 57).

Sky-reaching pose | **Hurdler's stretch** | **Cobra stretch**

belly day (cont'd)

MOVE 3: leg rolls with swiss ball
obliques

a. Lie on your back with your arms out to the sides and your palms against the floor. Grasp a fitness ball between your ankles with your legs extended toward the ceiling.

b. Exhale as you slowly lower your legs to the right. Try to keep both shoulder blades against the floor as you twist. Inhale as you return to the starting position, then exhale as you drop your legs to the left. Continue alternating between right and left for 1 minute, then move on to Move 4.

a

b

eat nutritionally, *not* emotionally® visualization

Today you will continue to cultivate your inner self-love through visualization, this time by seeing yourself from the perspective of someone who cares about you and admires you. Close your eyes and take a few deep, relaxing breaths, in through your nose and out through your mouth. Allow each exhalation to bring you to a state of deep relaxation. Once you feel completely relaxed, you're ready to begin.

MOVE 4: v-sit with swiss ball
lower rectus abdominus

a. Sit on the floor with your legs extended. Hold a fitness ball between your palms with your arms extended at chest level.

b. Exhale as you lean back slightly and lift your legs until you form a V-shape with your torso. Hold for up to 1 minute, then return to Move 1 on page 164. Repeat Moves 1–4 once more, and you're done.

a

b

you at center stage

Try to see yourself through the eyes of someone who really cares about you, such as a close friend, your spouse, or one of your children. Feel the same admiration that this person feels as you watch yourself through their eyes. Try to see all of the good qualities about yourself that *they* see every day.

Watch yourself from afar as your loved ones walk up to you and tell you how much they love and admire you. Watch your expression as they tell you about your good qualities. What do they say? Now imagine more and more people coming into the room and staring at you with the same love and admiration of your loved one. As the room fills with people, they begin to applause, clapping for you!

Level 3
Saturday

"We've got two
lives. The one we're
given and the one
we make."

—Kobe Yamada

jorge's power thought

Many people have asked me whether they should just focus on the Cruise Moves for their trouble area—their bellies—and omit the moves for the rest of their bodies. If you're wondering the same thing, the answer is a "No." You must target the muscles all over your body to give yourself the *metabolism boost* needed to burn the fat in your belly. Of course, you can certainly give your abdominal muscles some extra attention. That's why this program has you target your trouble area three times a week. But you should never try to spot tone by working only one body area. It just won't work.

"Recommit yourself to your goal. Remember: not only do you want a beautiful belly, but you also want to stick with your new healthy habits for life."

body cleanse
day off from cruise moves

Today is your day off from Cruise Moves, but not a day off from the program. Use today to pamper yourself inside and out. Spend some time relaxing—both your mind and body. Read that novel that you've been putting off. Spend some time at the park, writing in the journal provided on the opposite page. Or take a nap in the afternoon! This is your day to rest, relax, and rejuvenate, your day to completely cleanse your body.

To cleanse your body, follow my three-step plan:

1. Drink your psyllium shake for breakfast. The shake replaces your meal. Don't have anything for breakfast other than your shake. (To purchase psyllium husk powder, visit www.jorgecruise.com.)

2. Make both lunch and dinner's protein serving non-meat options. See the bonus chapter on page 319 for sample vegetable protein meals.

3. Drink eight 16-ounce glasses of water, doubling your usual water intake.

eat nutritionally, *not* emotionally®
visualization

During your last visualization, you learned how to cultivate love toward yourself. During this visualization you will learn how to cultivate love toward others, particularly those whom you experience difficulty getting along with. Close your eyes and take a few deep, relaxing breaths, in through your nose and out through your mouth. Allow each exhalation to bring you to a state of deep relaxation. Once you feel completely relaxed, you're ready to begin.

journal _____

_____   _____
_____   _____
_____   _____
_____   _____
_____   _____
_____   _____
_____   _____
_____   _____
_____   _____
_____   _____
_____   _____
_____   _____
_____   _____
_____   _____
_____   _____

loving your enemies

See in your mind the image of a person with whom you experience difficulty getting along. Rather than focusing on this person's negative qualities, however, focus on what makes this person endearing. At first, this may be difficult, but I know you can do it. Visualize this person's good qualities and virtues. Perhaps this person is a good listener or a hard worker. Try to remember a time when you got along with this person. Perhaps she was kind to you during a time of stress. Cultivate this memory in your mind and try to call up every detail. As you do so, feel a sense of love growing in your heart. End your visualization by wishing that this person stay free from suffering. You'll be surprised by how much your positive wishes affect your relationship for the better!

Level 3
Sunday

"We don't receive wisdom; we must discover it for ourselves after a journey that no one can take for us or spare us."

—**Marcel Proust**

jorge's power thought

With 300 calories and 30 grams of fat each, it's no wonder avocados have received a bad reputation. But here's the good news. Avocados are now being hailed by nutritional experts for their exceptional health benefits. It's true that avocados are high in fat, but the type of fat is a mostly heart-healthy monunsaturated fat (the good fat!). They contain lutein, which is vital for healthy vision; folic acid, which helps prevent birth defects; and a special substance that reduces the amount of cholesterol absorbed from food. New findings also show that avocados have nearly twice as much vitamin E—important for healthy muscles—than previously thought. So go ahead and put ⅛ of an avocado slice in your salad or spread a tablespoon of guacamole on your burrito for a delicious and healthy indulgence.

"Nothing in life is more amazing than finishing something that you've set your heart on. Your focus and dedication has helped you to change your body and your life."

capture your progress
day off from cruise moves

Today is your day off. Take a moment to relish your progress. Grab a pen and answer the following questions. Then share the answers with me by sending an e-mail to flatbelly3@jorgecruise.com.

1. What is your current weight?

_____

2. What was your original weight?

_____

3. What is your waist circumference in inches?

_____

4. What was your original waist circumference in inches?

_____

5. What have you done well this week? What are you most proud of?

_____

_____

_____

_____

_____

6. What could you improve next week?

_____

_____

_____

_____

_____

eat nutritionally, *not* emotionally®
visualization

Today we're going to take a trip into the future where you will hear a good friend describe you to someone who doesn't know you. Are you curious? Do the following visualization with me for just a few minutes. Close your eyes and take a few relaxing breaths, in through your nose and out through your mouth. Allow each exhalation to bring you to a state of deep relaxation. Once you feel completely relaxed, you're ready to begin.

judy thompson dropped four clothing sizes!

"Thanks to Jorge Cruise's 8 Minutes in the Morning program, I have lost 40 pounds and had to cinch my belt 6 inches smaller.

"Jorge's program makes the belly exercises extremely simple. No matter what difficulty level, each session takes hardly any time to complete. I most enjoyed the exercises from Level 2 that incorporated the use of the fitness ball. I find that I not only get the benefit of the specific exercise, but I also have the fun of trying to maintain my balance!

"I have been astonished by my results. I started at 205 pounds and now am down to 165. I don't even remember weighing this little. Jorge has shown me that I do have control over my life. I now have the confidence that I will maintain this weight. I now look forward to and enjoy getting dressed up. It is so nice to have people comment on my size and the appearance of my abdomen."

Judy Thompson shrunk
her waist 6 inches!

you—in someone else's words

Imagine you will soon be introduced to Joe, a buddy of your close friend, for the first time. Your friend and Joe have gotten together for coffee one day and your name has come up. Your friend says to Joe, "Oh yes, you have to meet her. She's a great friend and just a wonderful person." Joe asks, "What make's her so great?" What does your friend say about you? Does she talk about how you are always there with a smile when she needs you? Does she say that you are understanding and compassionate? Or steadfast and courageous? Or maybe that you have a great sense of humor or quick wit? When Joe asks what you look like, hear how your friend describes you, from your hair color to your toned legs, from your beauty mark to your great eyes. Smile, because you know your friend loves you very much.

Part 3

Lean Hips and Thin Thighs Program

Introduction

With Jorge's plan *I have lost 105 pounds and more than 12 inches off my thighs*. My 49th birthday present to myself was a professional picture taken of my granddaughter and me!

I feel like a new woman, I love being a young grandmother, and I'm looking forward to being "Fifty and Fit."

But I was not always this way. You see like many of you reading this, I have always been overweight. I have yo-yo'd on virtually every diet and have taken every over-the-counter diet aid. My weight has fluctuated my entire adult life—every time I lost weight I gained it—plus more!

In 1993, my family was in a tragic car crash. My oldest daughter broke her neck in two places, and my world as I knew it came to a screeching halt. I was driving when the accident happened, and the guilt was more than I could bear. Although my daughter never blamed me, I felt I needed to punish myself. As I have always been an emotional eater, I turned to food for comfort as it was always there for me. Sometimes the food felt very comforting, other times I used it as punishment.

Nancy changed her life and lost 12 inches off her thighs!

Over the years, I have watched in admiration as my daughter turned this horrible experience into a reason to live on, and live happily. She once told me the accident happened for a reason and that it gave her a path in life. That night I kept thinking, "Where is my path in life? To keep self-destructing?" At 5 feet tall my weight ballooned up to over 200 pounds.

In 2001, I was blessed with a beautiful, healthy granddaughter, Talia. I was given a reason to be happy, to enjoy life, but I continued to knowingly eat unhealthily and gained more weight. I avoided being in pictures and videos with my granddaughter.

I remember clearly, when Talia was 11 months old, I was sitting on the floor watching her and thinking, "I want her to be proud of me, not ashamed. I want to take her to the park; I want to be in pictures with her." I remember tears welling up and that is when I started my new healthy life. As things are meant to be, it was soon after that I saw Jorge Cruise on TV. Since using his 8-minute technique, I have gone from 225 pounds to 120 pounds.

I truly believe in Jorge's core philosophy that diets don't work and that the secret is to restore your resting metabolism by creating lean muscle. This plan will work for you . . . if you make the commitment.

My single most important tip to you right now so that you make a commitment that lasts is to believe in yourself. No matter what has happened in the past, no one can change your future but you. Find a blessing in your life, say "thank you," and work each day to fulfill your goals. Thank you, Talia, for giving me a reason to be healthy and enjoy life. . . . Thank you, Jorge, for giving me the tools to achieve my goals.

Nancy Bloom, JorgeCruise.com client

the nature of hip and thigh fat

Many women tell me that every stray calorie seems to migrate to their hips and thighs. This is not a figment of their imaginations.

Before menopause, many women's bodies store excess fat predominantly in the hips and thighs, creating what's come to be known as the "pear-shaped" body. Your body can easily mobilize this excess fat during pregnancy and breastfeeding, when the body needs as many as 1,000 extra calories a day. Fat storage in these sites dates back thousands of years, when it greatly helped certain cave-dwelling humans survive during times of drought and famine. Women who could easily store fat in their hips and thighs tended to be able to give birth and feed a baby during a drought, thus passing on their thigh-fat-storing genetics to future generations.

This is one reason why thigh fat is so difficult to get rid of. Genes left over from your cave-dwelling ancestors cause hormones and enzymes in your body to direct every extra calorie into waiting fat cells in your hips and thighs. For example, your levels of the female sex hormone estrogen may be a tad higher than other women whose bodies don't store excess fat in these areas (or as much of it).

But there are ways to coax these fat cells in your thighs to release their contents, and to coax your muscle cells into burning it up! So don't despair.

the causes of cellulite

Besides excess fat in their thighs, many women complain to me about a certain type of fat known as cellulite. They tell me that no matter how much weight they lose, they can't seem to smooth out the tiny lumps of fat on their thighs. Indeed, some of the most slender women have cellulite. As many as 85 percent of teenage girls have it.

Cellulite is created when fat manages to push its way through tiny holes in your connective tissue, the thick web of interwoven fibers just underneath your skin. Strong and healthy connective tissue forms a tighter web of interwoven fibers, preventing fat from pressing its way through. Weak, unhealthy connective tissue, on the other hand, more easily stretches apart, allowing tiny fat pockets to poke through. Many factors can weaken your connective tissue, setting the stage for cellulite. They include:

High hormone levels. Women with higher-than-normal levels of the female hormone estrogen tend to suffer more often from cellulite. Other than directing extra calories to fat cells in your thighs, estrogen also weakens connective tissue. When estrogen softens connective tissue around the womb, it makes childbirth possible. Unfortunately, estrogen softens *all* of the connective tissue in your body, not just that around your womb.

Poor blood circulation. Usually, high estrogen levels alone won't trigger cellulite to form. Many experts believe that you must also have poor blood circulation to your connective tissue, which tends to cause swelling. The swelling stretches the connective tissue apart, allowing the fat to bulge through.

Fluid retention. Many people think that fluid retention takes place only in the abdomen. That's not true. It actually occurs all over your body, including your thighs. If you've ever pulled on a favorite pair of pants and found them tight in the thighs on one day and loose on the next, you've experienced the ebb and flow of fluid retention. Any type of swelling in your thighs—particularly on a chronic basis—will stretch out and weaken connective tissue.

A frenzied lifestyle. Emotional stress has been shown to weaken connective tissue. My *8 Minutes in the Morning for a Perfect Body* program will help you smooth away cellulite in many ways. First, daily exercise will help to normalize your hormonal levels. This not only helps prevent cellulite, it will also help to prevent mood swings.

Second, my Cruise Moves exercise program will increase blood circulation to your thighs, helping to keep the connective tissue healthy. Better blood circulation will, in turn, help to remove excess fluid. Finally, as you shed fat in your hips and thighs, you'll have less of it to press against your connective tissue.

some good news and some bad news

Genetically speaking, there are two predominant body types. Some people gain fat in their lower bodies, creating the pear shape mentioned earlier. And

Frequently Asked Questions

Here are some questions that I often get from clients about their hips and thighs.

I've been doing lots of leg exercises, but it seems like my thighs are getting bigger and bigger. What's going on?

To slim down your thighs, you must build muscle all over your body to boost your metabolism to burn the fat. Doing lots of leg lifts will only build muscle in your legs, but won't burn the fat. As the muscle grows, your legs will grow. You must burn the fat to shrink the size of your thighs. My program will help you to do just that.

It seems like every time I go on a diet, my upper body shrinks, but my lower body doesn't budge. Why does this happen?

The only way to shrink your lower body without shrinking your upper body is to stop dieting! Dieting sends your body into starvation mode. To help you survive the famine, your body preferentially burns fat in your upper body and conserves the fat in your lower body. The more often you diet, the more pronounced this problem will become. The only way to burn fat in your lower body is to stop dieting and start strength training!

Everyone in my family has big thighs. Slimming my thighs is a hopeless battle, isn't it?

That couldn't be farther from the truth. You may have inherited the tendency to store fat in your thighs from your parents, but that doesn't mean you can't burn the fat! Stick with me and you'll soon be a believer.

still others tend to gain fat in their abdomens, creating what's known as an apple shape.

Though you may have come to despise the fat on your hips and thighs, you should know that you have a major advantage over people who tend to gain it elsewhere. Research has shown over and over again that abdominal fat—and not hip and thigh fat—is particularly dangerous to your health. Abdominal fat more easily makes its way into your bloodstream, clogging your arteries. Thigh fat is much less likely to do so.

Now for the bad news. Thigh fat is a little harder to burn off than belly fat. You probably know this already. If you and a boyfriend, guy friend, or husband have ever resolved to lose weight at the same time, you probably noticed that he had a much easier time dropping the weight in his belly than you did in your thighs.

Regardless, that doesn't mean you can't burn it off.

I know that women who have excess thigh fat are generally the most motivated to get rid of it. So I probably don't have to give you much of a pep talk to help motivate you toward your goal.

Abdominal fat is easy to hide with a big sweater. Thigh fat, on the other hand, is almost impossible to hide. And summer can be a very difficult time for women. My female friends and online clients tell me that they hate wearing shorts and swimsuits because they hate revealing their legs. And they tell me that their pants tend to hug too tightly in the thighs.

But you are going to change all of that! We are going to slim down those thighs and hips and smooth away that cellulite, creating a beautiful, sexy body from head to toe. Have you always wanted to wear those low-rider jeans but

Diane Sutherlin lost 4 inches!

I went from a size 14–16 pant size to a size 10. I have lost 21 pounds and feel so much better about myself. I feel better not only because I have dropped the weight but also because I feel I have so much more control over my life. I realize that I have choices and I am no longer a victim to food. I don't have to give up my favorite things; I just have them in smaller quantities. I am proud to say that I am over halfway to my goal and that I have learned other ways to cope with my stress than turning to food. Jorge has taught me some lifelong tools that I will always be able to fall back on in those difficult moments.

Diane dropped 3 pants sizes!

shunned them because they were too tight in the thighs? You'll be able to after finishing this *8 Minutes in the Morning for a Perfect Body* program. You'll be able to confidently bare your legs in shorts and swimsuits. Your thighs will no longer rub together when you walk.

And those are just the visual benefits. The muscles in your legs are some of the largest and strongest muscles in your body.

Stronger leg muscles make your overall life feel so much more effortless. You'll walk with more confidence and a spring in your step. You'll be able to climb stairs without getting tired. And you'll be able to go on strenuous hikes—all because of your strong legs!

You will feel better about yourself from the inside out. And isn't that really what it's all about? Sure, you will look

better. But you'll feel fantastic! **So promise me right now that you will make the commitment to sticking with the program.** Promise me—and promise yourself—that you will find 8 minutes each day to complete your morning moves. Once you've made your promise, turn back to chapter 2 to find out more about the magic of the 8 Minutes in the Morning program.

Chapter 6
8 Minute Moves

the magic 8 minute ingredient

Now that you understand why lean muscle is so important to your success, you're ready to find out how to create it. You're going to take your first step forward on your journey to lean hips and thin thighs by learning about focused Cruise Moves.

These unique resistance-training exercises will help you to create the lean muscle needed to burn the fat in your lower body. Cruise Moves provide the magic 8 minute ingredient to help you thin down your thighs and create leaner hips. Cruise Moves are the most efficient, effective, and convenient way to create lean muscle. They involve no aerobics and no trips to the gym. They take just 8 minutes each morning. And they're simple and easy to learn.

Cruise Moves will help you to sculpt beautiful long and lean muscle in your thighs and elsewhere. That lean muscle tissue will rev up your metabolism, helping you to incinerate excess fat. It will also help you tone and firm your hips and thighs,

along with the rest of your body. With the help of Cruise Moves, your thighs will appear longer, leaner, and sexier. You'll want to show them off everywhere you go!

your weekly schedule

In chapter 7, on pages 198 to 317, you will find three Cruise Moves programs, ranging from very gentle to very challenging:

Level 1. The Cruise Moves for this level involve absolutely no equipment other than the chairs or pillows available in your home. They are very gentle and perfect for anyone starting a new exercise program for the first time, including former professional couch potatoes.

Level 2. These Cruise Moves are slightly more challenging than Level 1. They, too, involve no equipment.

Level 3. The Cruise Moves at this level are the most challenging and involve the use of ankle weights, which are available at any sporting goods store.

No matter your current fitness level, I suggest you start with Level 1. Follow Level 1 for 3 weeks before moving on to Level 2. Then do that program for 3 weeks before moving on to Level 3. Three weeks will give your body the time it needs to adapt to the Cruise Moves.

your "8 minute" edge

Unlike other resistance-training programs, your Cruise Moves sessions:

• Take only 8 minutes a day to complete

• Require minimal equipment

• Can be done in your own home, even while wearing your PJs.

Within 3 weeks, you will have built enough muscle to allow you to tackle the next level with ease.

(*Note:* Level 1 may feel too easy for some of you right away. If you don't feel challenged by the exercises, move up to Level 2 after just 1 week with Level 1.)

For every level of the program, you will follow the same schedule. (Consult "Your Cruise Moves Schedule" on page 186.) You'll target your hips and thighs on Mondays, Wednesdays, and Fridays with focused Cruise Moves for your lower body. On Tuesdays your Cruise Moves will target your upper body. On Thursdays they'll target your torso and calves.

Sometimes people ask me if they can skip the Cruise Moves on Tuesdays and Thursdays. "My trouble zone is my lower half, not my upper half," they sometimes comment. I always tell them, as I am telling you right now, that you must create lean muscle *all over your body*—not just in your legs—in order to boost your metabolism high enough to see real results. Here's another important reason to tone your upper body: Many pear-shaped women have very skinny shoulders and arms, which make their hips seem even wider. Resistance-training exercises will help to fill out your shoulders, creating more balance between your

shoulders and hips and helping to make your waist look smaller.

Here's another question that I often hear. Many people ask me whether they can speed their results by working their hips and thighs *every day*. The answer to that is a strong *NO*. You must give your muscles 48 hours to recover between sessions. That's when the true magic happens. During your time off from your hips and thighs routine, your muscles recover and grow stronger. If you work your hips and thighs every day—and you never give them a chance to re-cover—your muscles can never regenerate. Instead of speeding up your metabolism, you may instead slow it down. You'll end up feeling fatigued and you can even get injured.

The bottom line is that you achieve better results faster by targeting your trouble zone 3 days a week instead of 5 or more. Remember: When it comes to weight loss, less effort often produces more results! That's part of the Jorge Cruise® revolution.

a word about weekends

Each weekend you will get 2 days off from your Cruise Moves. On Saturdays, I recom-

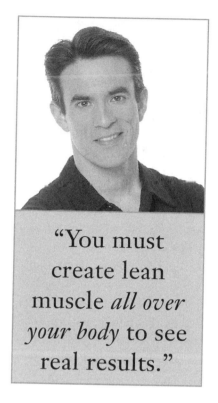

"You must create lean muscle *all over your body* to see real results."

mend that you spend your 8 minutes in the morning doing a set of stretches that will help lengthen your hip and thigh muscles. Don't misunderstand me. My Cruise Moves will help you to create long, lean muscles, not thick, bulky ones. However, these Saturday stretches will *accelerate* your results by helping to lengthen your leg muscles even more.

Whenever you stretch, you not only help increase your flexibility, but you also elongate your muscles. If you stretch often enough, your muscles will remain longer. And here's another good reason to stretch. It helps increase circulation to your muscles. This added circulation will help you to feel good, stretching away any tightness that may have developed during the week. It also may help reduce the appearance of cellulite. Stretching helps to improve the health of your connective tissue. Remember in chapter 1 when I told you about those tiny holes in connective tissue that allow small amounts of fat to bulge through, creating the bumpy appearance that we've come to call cellulite? Regular stretching helps your connective tissue stay healthy, closing up those gaps and preventing the fat from bulging through.

If you already have a set of stretches that you love to do, that's great. Go ahead and do them. If not, you'll find my favorite stretches in the bonus chapter on page 194.

Each Sunday, you have the day off. You have no stretches and no Cruise Moves in the morning. I suggest that you use Sundays to record your progress: Weigh yourself and measure your hip and thigh circumferences.

Try to use Sundays as a true respite from the week. Make it your time to relax and rejuvenate. Many of my clients tell me

that they like to set aside some time each Sunday to plan and prepare for the week ahead. You might chop up some veggies to use during the week for lunch or plan your dinner menus and make sure you have healthy food on hand. Do whatever you need to do to make sure your week goes smoothly—you'll increase your chances of sticking to your morning moves and your Cruise Down Plate, which you learned about in chapter 3.

the format for each day

No matter what, the format for your day will be the same. You will wake up and do whatever you need to do to ready yourself for your morning moves. Some of my clients tell me that after a trip to the bathroom, they like to splash some water on their faces, drink a glass of water, and brush their teeth. After that, they are ready to move.

Each morning during the week you will find four Cruise Moves. **You will do each move for 1 minute and then move on to the next move. Once you have finished all four moves, you will repeat each move one time for 1 minute each—for a total of 8 minutes.** *It's that easy.*

How can you complete a session so quickly? I've strategically paired your Cruise Moves so that you will always be working opposing muscle groups. For example, when you target your inner thigh, your outer thigh gets to rest. When you target your outer thigh, your inner thigh gets to rest. I call this *Active Rest Moves*®. That way, you never need to rest between moves. There's no wasted time on the 8 Minutes program. You simply transition from move to move for 8 minutes. It's a focused program that works!

your cruise moves schedule

Here's what you will be doing each day on the *8 Minutes in the Morning for a Perfect Body* program.
monday: Hips and Thighs
tuesday: Chest, Upper Back, Biceps, Triceps
wednesday: Hips and Thighs
thursday: Belly, Low Back, Shoulders, Calves
friday: Hips and Thighs
saturday: Muscle Lengthening and Stretching
sunday: Day Off: Assess Your Progress

how you'll address your trouble zone

Now here's where things get really exciting. If you've tried to slim down your hips and thighs in the past, you may have noticed that particular exercises seem to make your hips and thighs larger! That usually happens when you solely focus on just one area of the thigh.

Well, you'll be happy to hear that there is a mix of moves in this book. These moves are sorted into four thigh zones.

Here are the four zones you will target 3 days a week.

Inner thighs. The muscles along your inner thighs are collectively known as your adductors, because the are responsible for "adducting" or pulling your legs in toward the centerline of your body. Toning these muscles will not only help keep your inner thighs from jiggling, but also will help to pull your inner thighs closer to your thigh bone, shrinking their appearance and preventing them from rubbing together when you walk.

Front of the thighs. The muscles along the front of your thighs are collectively called your quadriceps and hip flexors. They help you to extend and lift your leg forward.

Outer thighs and hips. The muscles that are on your outer thighs and hips are collectively called your abductors because they "abduct" or lift your leg away from the centerline of your body. (Think of the quintessential leg lift.) Along your hips, the most important abductor is the gluteus medius. Toning this muscle, along with your other abductors, will help smooth away saddlebags. These muscles also help to hold your kneecap in place, so training them will help to prevent knee pain.

Backs of the thighs and rear end. A number of different muscles make up the backside of your leg. Along the back of your thigh are a group of muscles called your hamstrings. In your buttocks, there's the gluteus maximus. Your hamstrings and gluteus maximus work together to help lift your leg back behind your torso. Your hamstrings also help you to bend your knee. Toning your hamstrings will help smooth out the back of your thigh and reduce the appearance of cellulite. It also will help to provide separation between your thigh and butt. Toning your gluteus will help lift your butt cheeks.

"When it comes to resistance training, less time often produces more results!"

why you should move in the morning

Once you understand the power of exercising in the morning, you'll never go back to afternoon or evening workouts.

First, when you move in the morning, you're more likely to feel good for the rest of the day. You feel stronger, more energized, and less stressed. In a study at the University of Leeds in England, researchers found that women who exercised in the morning reported less tension and greater feelings of contentment for the rest of the day than those who didn't exercise in the morning. When you do your Cruise Moves, you send a signal to your pituitary gland to release endorphins, your body's natural feel-good chemicals. The more endorphins you have in your bloodstream, the better you feel. Thanks to morning exercise, you will be able to better handle stress no matter what happens in your day.

But that's not all. Moving in the morning also helps you to shed fat faster than moving at other times of the day. When you first wake up, your metabolism is sluggish because it has slowed down during sleep. But when you exercise, your metabolism increases. By doing your Cruise Moves first thing in the morning, you boost your metabolism when it's normally the slowest. You're also better able to build lean muscle when you move in the morning. Resting levels of testosterone, the body's primary muscle-building hormone, are the highest in the morning. This suggests that the muscle-creating potential of resistance training may be at its peak before noon.

In short, you burn more calories when you exercise in the morning, making better use of your exercise time.

Finally, moving in the morning

just sleep on it

Many of my clients give me a funny look when I tell them that an **extra hour** of sleep at night could help them to lose weight faster. Here's why sleep is so important to your success. It's during deep, stage 4 sleep that your body repairs and regenerates itself. During stage 4 sleep your body secretes growth hormone, a protein used to repair muscles and injured tissues. If you don't spend enough time in stage 4 sleep, this important body repair process doesn't fully complete itself.

In fact, researchers suspect that people who have chronic pain syndromes like fibromyalgia don't spend enough time in stage 4 sleep. In experiments done in the 1970s, it took just a week of light sleeping—where people were not allowed to enter stage 4 sleep—before muscle aches and pains popped up.

Other research has found that getting just 1 hour too little of sleep can lower levels of the hormone testosterone. Though more abundant in men, both men and women have this hormone, important in the muscle-creating process. When you don't have enough testosterone, it throws off your muscle-to-fat ratio, promoting fat storage and hindering muscle development.

Not getting enough sleep can also cause depression and bad moods, which can lead to overeating. It also lowers your immunity, which can lead to colds that force you to skip your Cruise Moves sessions. Finally, when you go to bed on time, you're more likely to get out of bed on time—in time to do your Cruise Moves.

Surveys show that only about one-third of people sleep at least 8 hours. Promise me that you will make sleep a priority. Turn off the TV and head to bed at a reasonable hour. Your body and thighs will thank you.

helps you to stay consistent. Have you ever *planned* to exercise in the afternoon or evening only to skip those plans because something else came up? That usually doesn't happen first thing in the morning. Simply put, your morning is *your* time. It's the easiest time to control. You can roll out of bed, do your moves, and have some extra time just for you.

Later in the day, distractions will come up. Your spouse, your children, your job, or an emergency will interrupt your plans and force you to put your Cruise Moves on hold. Research shows that only 25 percent of evening exercisers consistently do their exercise routines, compared to 75 percent of morning exercisers. The bottom line is that when you commit to exercising in the morning, you bypass excuses and shed the pounds faster because you are more consistent.

8 minutes is all you need

So now that you understand how Cruise Moves will slim down your hips and thighs, I ask you to promise yourself that you will commit to 8 minutes each morning. That's all you need—just 8 minutes. I'm not asking for 20 or 30 or 45. *Just 8 minutes.* So set your alarm to wake you 8 minutes earlier and start going to bed earlier at night. And then turn to chapter 3 to find out about the next important step in your journey to lean hips and thin thighs.

"When you commit to exercising in the morning, you bypass excuses and shed the pounds faster."

Chapter 7

Putting the Jorge Cruise® Plan into Action

Use This 3-Level Plan to Slim Your Hips and Thighs

getting ready

Welcome to your *8 Minutes in the Morning for a Perfect Body* program. This is where the rubber meets the road, so to speak, because you will be putting everything you've just learned into action.

In the following pages you'll find three different programs, ranging in difficulty from gentle to challenging.

Start with Level 1, the gentlest of the programs. Each program starts on a Monday and ends on a Sunday. You'll repeat each program for 3 weeks before moving onto the next level. In other words, you'll start Level 1 on a Monday and follow it for 21 days, starting over each Monday. After 21 days, you'll advance to Level 2. After 21 more days, you'll advance to Level 3.

If you are already fairly fit, Level 1 may feel too easy for you. If you don't feel challenged by the exercises, you may move up to Level 2 after just one week.

how to use the program

Each day during your Monday through Friday sessions, you will find a power thought to help keep you motivated, four Cruise Moves, and a visualization that will help you to eat nutritionally and not emotionally.

Always start your morning with your Cruise Moves—they are the core of the program and your most important ally in slimming your hips and thighs. Your sessions Monday, Wednesday, and Friday will focus on your trouble zone—your hips and thighs. Your Tuesday sessions will focus on your upper body and your Thursday sessions will target your midsection and calves.

Warm up by jogging in place for 1 minute. Then do each Cruise Move for 1 minute and then move on to the next Cruise Move. After you've completed all four moves, repeat each move one time for a total of 8 minutes. Then cool down with the stretches suggested on page 194.

Each day of the program you will find a powerful visualization to help you overcome emotional eating and stay motivated. When you create an image in your mind of what you want to accomplish, you take the first crucial step to making your dreams a reality. The visualizations in this program will help you more effectively deal with negative emotions that may have caused you to overeat in the past, confront difficult people and situations that

a 2-step format

Each day of the program follows a simple format. Each day you do two things:

Step 1.
8 Minutes Moves®
(Cruise Moves)

Step 2.
Eat Nutritionally, *Not* Emotionally®

sometimes trigger mood swings, and build a strong internal motivation to follow a healthful diet.

During your visualizations, you need to draw on all of your senses: touch, taste, smell, sight, and sound. The more senses you involve in your visualizations, the more powerful your images will become and the more effective your time spent.

how weekends work

You will tackle your weekends a little differently than your Monday through Friday sessions. You'll take each weekend off from your Cruise Moves, but not from building lean muscle and taking additional steps toward your goal. Each Saturday you will find four stretches for the hip and thigh zone. These stretches will help *elongate* your

muscles. They are an optional component of the program. However, they take only 8 minutes, and they will greatly *accelerate* your results. (You'll find additional optional ways to accelerate your results in the bonus chapter on page 319.)

Each Sunday you will also take the day off from Cruise Moves. However, take a moment to capture your progress by weighing yourself and taking your hip and thigh measurements. Also, feel free to enjoy your stronger body by taking a hike, playing a game of Frisbee, or taking your kids for a walk at the park.

your homework

Before you get started on your new adventure, you'll need to make sure you have the tools for the journey. Please don't start the program until you:

1. Purchase your equipment. You need minimal equipment for *8 Minutes in the Morning for a Perfect Body*. When you get to Level 3, I suggest you try the hips and legs exercises with a pair of ankle weights, available at most sporting goods stores and at JorgeCruise.com. These small weights easily strap to your ankles and will help add resistance, making your Cruise Moves more effective.

2. Read chapters 1 through 3. Please don't start the program without first reading about how it works and understanding the formula behind the 2-step process.

3. Write down your current weight and measurements and take a "before" photo. Your original weight, hips and thighs circumference, and before photo will not only help serve as powerful reminders of your goal, but they will also help you to see your progress. To take your measurements, use a flexible tape measure. Wrap it around your hips at their widest point. Then do the same with your thighs, wrapping it around your thigh roughly mid-distance between your knee and hipbone. Record your measurements and weight in the space provided on the opposite page.

4. Determine your goal. Sure, you want leaner hips and thinner thighs, but how much leaner?

How many pounds down? I recommend you pick a goal weight. That way you'll know when you've reached your goal! To pick a goal weight, consult the height and weight chart on the opposite page. Find your age on the chart and match that to your height. There you will find a healthy weight range for someone your age and size. Use that to determine your goal. Write your goal in the space provided.

You also might want to choose a motivational goal as well, one that is not tied to the scale. For example, do you have a pair of jeans that you can no longer wear? You might want to write that down as a goal, too.

5. Determine how long it will take to reach your goal. You'll find out how to do just that by consulting the chart on the opposite page.

your cooldown stretches

After your Cruise Moves, do the following stretches to cool down and increase your flexibility.

Sky-reaching pose. Stand tall and reach with both hands toward the sky as high as you comfortably can. Feel the stretch lengthening your spine, bringing more range of motion to your joints. Breathe deeply through your nose. Hold from 10 seconds to 1 minute.

Cobra stretch. Lie on a towel or mat on your belly with your palms flat on the ground next to your shoulders and your legs just slightly less than shoulder-width apart. Your feet should be resting on their tops. Lift your upper body up

off the ground, inhaling through your nose as you rise. Press your hips into the floor and curve your upper body backward, looking up. This stretch is one that you may need to work up to, so right now, do the best you can. Hold from 10 seconds to 1 minute.

Hurdler's stretch. Sit on a towel or mat on the floor with your legs extended in front of you. Keeping your back straight, gently bend forward from the hips and reach as far as you can toward your toes. If possible, pull your toes back slightly toward your upper body. Again, don't worry if this stretch is difficult for you right now—do the best you can. Eventually, you'll get it! Hold from 10 seconds to 1 minute.

your current body and future goals

To find your healthy weight, find your age and height on the chart below. You know yourself better than anyone else does, so select a number that is realistic for you. Subtract that number from your current weight. That's your weight-loss goal.

Then, to determine a target date for achieving this goal, divide your goal weight by two. That's the number of weeks it will take to reach your goal. Consult a calendar and find the date you will achieve your goal weight, then record your answers to the following:

1. What is your current weight? _____
2. What is your current thigh circumference in inches? _____
3. What is your current hip circumference in inches? _____

your future body

1. What is your goal weight? _____
2. How many weeks will it take to reach your goal weight? _____
3. What is your goal thigh circumference in inches? _____
4. What is your goal hip circumference in inches? _____
5. List any other goals: _____

your weight chart

Height (ft/in.)	Weight (lb) 19–34 yr	35+ yr	Height (ft/in.)	Weight (lb) 19–34 yr	35+ yr
5'0"	97–128	108–38	5'8"	125–64	138–78
5'1"	101–32	111–43	5'9"	129–69	142–83
5'2"	104–37	115–48	5'10"	132–74	146–88
5'3"	107–41	119–52	5'11"	136–79	151–94
5'4"	111–46	122–57	6'0"	140–84	155–99
5'5"	114–50	126–62	6'1"	144–89	159–205
5'6"	118–55	130–67	6'2"	148–95	164–210
5'7"	121–60	134–72	6'3"	152–200	168–216

SOURCE: U.S. Department of Health and Human Services, Dietary Guidelines for Americans

MY "BEFORE" AND "AFTER" PHOTOS

Your "before" and "after" photos will help motivate you to stay focused on your weight-loss goal.
Review this page each day to *prevent* emotional eating. Take your "before" photo
right now and paste it on this page. But don't wait to see your future body!
Go to www.jorgecruise.com/futurebody and print out your "after" photo right now.
Photocopy this page for each day of the program and use it to keep yourself organized.

Before Photo Front View

After Photo Front View

Instructions for using the planner: Make seven copies for each week. Then, stack them and staple in the upper left-hand corner. Keep them with you at all times.

JORGE CRUISE®
LEAN HIP & THIN THIGH PLANNER

Date _____

Step 1: 8 Minutes Moves®

Muscle-Making Routine:

Monday: Hips and Thighs Day
Tuesday: Upper Body
Wednesday: Hips and Thighs Day
Thursday: Lower Body
Friday: Hips and Thighs Day
Saturday: Stretch Day
Sunday: Day Off

	Set 1	Set 2
Move 1:		
Move 2:		
Move 3:		
Move 4:		

In each "Move" box, write down the Cruise Move® and then in the "Set 1 and Set 2" box, keep track of the number of reps performed or time held.

Step 2: Eat Nutritionally, *Not* Emotionally®

Muscle-Making Material:

Veggies: Salad, Steamed Veggies, or 1 Fruit
Fat: 1 tsp of Flax, Olive Oil, or Butter
Carbs: ½ cup of a grain or 1 slice of bread
Protein: 1 oz of Fish/Chicken/Meat/Cheese,
   3 Egg Whites, ½ cup of Beans, or 1 Glass of 1% Milk
Snacks: 100-calorie Item
Treat: 30- to 50-calorie Item

Each box equals an above example. Eat every 3 hours and stop eating 3 hours before bed.

Breakfast

Veggies/Fruit _____
Fat _____
Carbs _____
Protein _____

Snack

Lunch

Veggies/Fruit _____
Fat _____
Carbs _____
Protein _____

Snack

Dinner

Veggies/Fruit _____
Fat _____
Carbs _____
Protein _____
Treat _____

Water (✔): 8-oz Glass

○ ○ ○ ○
○ ○ ○ ○

www.jorgecruise.com

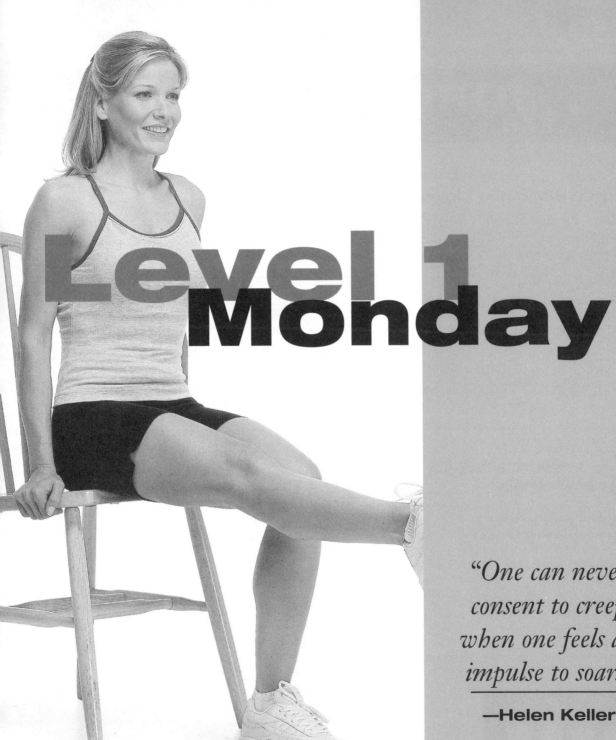

Level 1
Monday

"One can never
consent to creep
when one feels an
impulse to soar."

—Helen Keller

jorge's power thought

Today you take an important step forward toward your goal of leaner hips and thinner thighs. I want you to congratulate yourself for getting this far. Often getting started is half the battle. The other half of the battle? Sticking with it.

You may know from personal experience that losing weight and slimming down is only part of the effort. Staying that way and preventing weight gain is the other part. The way to keep the weight off? Make a commitment today that you will stick with this program for good! *8 Minutes in the Morning for a Perfect Body* is not a temporary fix for your body. Rather, it's a lifestyle. So stop thinking thoughts such as, "I only need to keep this up for 4 weeks." You must maintain it for life!

And here's some great news. The *8 Minutes in the Morning for a Perfect Body* program is the easiest program to keep up. My clients often tell me how it has become an integral part of their lives. No program is easier and more convenient. So make the commitment now, on day 1 of your journey, to make that lifestyle change and become a Jorge Cruise® client for life!

"You only need 8 minutes a day to slim down and stay that way. It's the most effective 8 minutes you can ever spend on your body."

8 minute moves®
thighs day

MOVE 1: seated pillow squeeze
inner thighs

a. Sit on a sturdy chair (one without wheels).
Rest your feet on the floor with your knees
bent at 90-degree angles. Place a pillow
between your thighs. Exhale as you squeeze
the pillow between your thighs, as if you were
trying to squeeze the stuffing out of the pillow.
Hold for 1 minute as you breathe normally.
Release and proceed to Move 2.

a

8-MINUTE LOG				
exercise	move 1	move 2	move 3	move 4
sets				
reps				

MOVE 2: seated hand push
outer thighs and hips

a. Sit on a sturdy chair. Rest your feet on the floor with your knees bent at 90-degree angles. Place your palms on the outsides of your knees. While keeping your palms and arms stationary, push your knees outward against your palms, as if you were trying to push your palms away. At the same time, press inward with your hands, preventing your thighs from pushing them outward. Hold this isometric contraction for 1 minute, breathing normally. Release and proceed to Move 3 on page 202.

a

exercise sequence

1. warm up Jog or march in place for 1 minute.

2. cruise moves Do one 60-second repetition of each of your 4 Cruise Moves. Repeat this cycle and you will be done in 8 minutes.

3. cool down After your Cruise Moves, do these stretches (see page 194).

Sky-reaching pose | Hurdler's stretch | Cobra stretch

thighs day (cont'd)

MOVE 3: seated leg raise
fronts of the thighs

a. Sit on a sturdy chair. Rest your feet on the floor with your knees bent at 90-degree angles. Rest your hands on the chair at your sides. Exhale as you lift and extend your right leg. Hold for 30 seconds as you breathe normally. Then inhale as you lower your right leg and exhale as you repeat with your left leg. Hold for 30 seconds while breathing normally. Release and proceed to Move 4.

a

eat nutritionally, *not* emotionally®
visualization

To help make sure you eat nutritionally and not emotionally, you can use a powerful mind-body technique called vivid visualization to help you stay emotionally strong and empowered. Today's visualization will help you fill up the void in your heart that may be leading to overeating. To begin, close your eyes and take a few deep, relaxing breaths in through your nose, out through your mouth. Allow each exhalation to bring you to a state of deep relaxation. Once you feel completely relaxed, you're ready to begin.

MOVE 4: seated bridge
backs of the thighs and rear end

a. Sit on the edge of a sturdy chair. Rest your feet on the floor with your knees bent at 90-degree angles. Rest your palms on the chair at your sides. Exhale as you lift your hips, allowing your palms and feet to support your body weight. Continue to lift your hips until your body resembles the shape of a bridge. Hold for 20 to 60 seconds while breathing normally. Release and return to Move 1 on page 200. Repeat Moves 1–4 once more, and you're done.

a

filling your void

Imagine a group of loving and compassionate people—ones you know in real life, or religious and historical figures—gathered with you. Imagine that they merge together to form a sphere of bright, warm, healing energy. See this energy move into your heart, filling it with love. Now, imagine that your heart glows and radiates love and that this radiating, warm light fills up every space so that your heart feels warm, full, and content.

Allow this loving energy to transcend the confines of your heart and fill up your entire body. As it fills up every nook and cranny, feel any negativity—anger, sadness, fear—become squeezed out of your body. Feel yourself grow happy, joyful, and content.

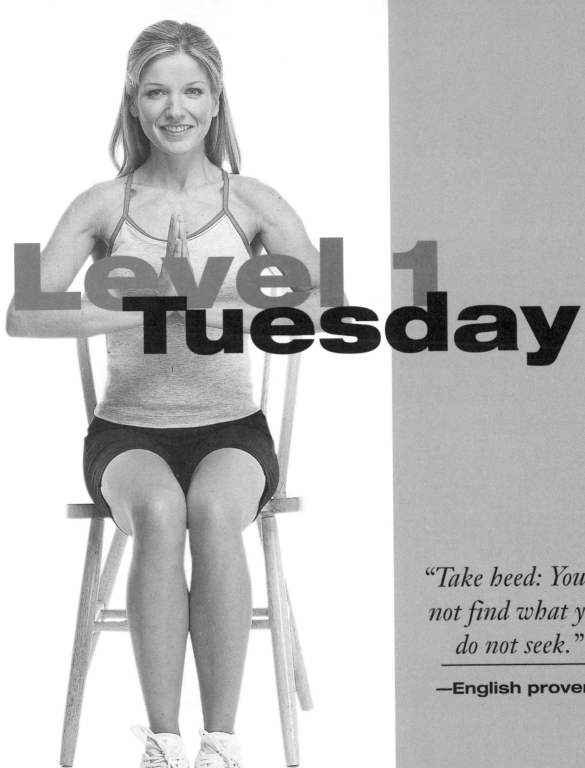

Level 1
Tuesday

"Take heed: You do not find what you do not seek."

—English proverb

jorge's power thought

Don't feel tempted to skip your Cruise Moves today. I know the reasoning. You might be thinking, "My true trouble zone is my thighs. I targeted them yesterday, so I might as well take off today." Don't let such thoughts talk you into hitting the snooze button on your alarm clock! Believe me, your 8 minutes in the morning today are better spent doing your Cruise Moves than sleeping!

As I've mentioned before, you must create muscle all over your body—including your arms, shoulders, chest, and back—to see true, lasting results. It's the muscle that you create all over your body that helps boost your metabolism high enough to burn the excess fat in your hips and thighs. If you target only your trouble zone, you won't slim your thighs. Also, your Cruise Moves for the upper body will help lift your breasts (if you're a woman) and firm underarm flab, a trouble spot for most people. Today's moves will help you shape strong, sexy arms and shoulders. They are crucial to your success.

So promise me right now that you will treat your non-trouble zone Cruise Moves today with the respect they deserve. Again, it's the best 8 minutes you will ever spend on your body. So get out of bed and get moving!

"Accept and nurture your body. Only then will nutrition and exercise efforts become effortless."

8 minute moves®
upper-body day

MOVE 1: squeeze hold
chest

a. Sit in a sturdy chair (one without wheels) with your feet flat on the floor. Bend your arms and exhale as you press the palms of your hands together at chest level. Once in position, keep your chest tight and flexed. Hold firmly for 60 seconds as you breathe normally, then proceed to Move 2.

a

8-MINUTE LOG				
exercise	move 1	move 2	move 3	move 4
sets				
reps				

MOVE 2: pull down hold
upper back

a. Sit 2 to 3 feet in front of a table in a sturdy chair with your feet flat on the floor. Bend forward from your hips and extend your arms onto the top of the table, placing your palms against the tabletop. Exhale as you press down onto the table. Hold firmly for 60 seconds as you breathe normally, then proceed to Move 3 on page 208.

a

exercise sequence

1. warm up Jog or march in place for 1 minute.

2. cruise moves Do one 60-second repetition of each of your 4 Cruise Moves. Repeat this cycle and you will be done in 8 minutes.

3. cool down After your Cruise Moves, do these stretches (see page 194).

Sky-reaching pose | **Hurdler's stretch** | **Cobra stretch**

upper-body day (cont'd)

MOVE 3: push down hold
biceps

a. Sit about 2 feet away from a table in a sturdy chair with your feet flat on the floor. Place your palms on the table with your elbows bent about 90 degrees. Exhale as you press down into the tabletop as hard as you can. Hold for 60 seconds, breathing normally. Release and proceed to Move 4.

a

eat nutritionally, *not* emotionally®
visualization

Today you will continue to nurture your heart with another visualization exercise, helping to fill up any void that may lead to overeating. Close your eyes and take a few deep, relaxing breaths, in through your nose and out through your mouth. Feel your body relax more every time you exhale. Once you feel completely relaxed, you're ready to start.

MOVE 4: lift hold
triceps

a. Sit about 2 feet away from a table in a sturdy chair with your feet flat on the floor. Place your palms under the tabletop with your elbows bent about 90 degrees. Push up on the underside of the table as hard as you can. Hold firmly for 60 seconds, breathing normally. Release and return to Move 1 on page 206. Repeat Moves 1–4 once more, and you're done.

a

unconditional love

Imagine someone who loves you or loved you very deeply in the past, (It's okay if you choose someone who has passed away.) You might think of a parent or spouse or sibling or good friend. This person loves you unconditionally. Notice every feature of his or her face. Recall a time when this person displayed an act of unconditional love toward you. Recall every detail of this memory. Remember how it felt to let someone love and nurture you. Allow your heart to feel grateful for this loving memory.

Now explore how your heart feels. Did the love from this person help to fill up your heart? Allow your heart to open up and enjoy the love that you've just created.

Level 1
Wednesday

"There are no shortcuts to any place worth going."

—Unknown

jorge's power thought

From working with millions of online clients, I've learned that you must first accept your body—with all of its quirks and inconveniences—before you can change your body. I've also learned that people who want to improve their hip and thigh zone often most need this advice.

Take a moment to reflect upon your feelings about your body. How do you feel about your hips and thighs? Often when I ask my clients this question, a whole slew of negative thoughts pop up for them. Such nasty thoughts can unravel your best intentions. They erode your self-confidence and motivation to succeed. That's why you must get past those thoughts to experience true, lasting results.

How do you get past thinking negatively about your body shape? One of my clients developed what I now call the "Oops" technique. Whenever you find yourself thinking something like, "My thighs are hideous," or "Even an elephant has slimmer legs than me," just say "Oops" out loud. It may sound silly, but it helps to remind you to stop such negative thoughts and return your thinking to the positive. Remember, your hips and thighs are a precious gift. They allow you to walk! What would you do without them?

"If you don't fully accept your body, you will never treat it as the most precious gift that has ever been given to you."

8 minute moves®
thighs day

MOVE 1: seated pillow squeeze
inner thighs

a. Sit on a sturdy chair (one without wheels). Rest your feet on the floor with your knees bent at 90-degree angles. Place a pillow between your thighs. Exhale as you squeeze the pillow between your thighs, as if you were trying to squeeze the stuffing out of the pillow. Hold for 1 minute as you breathe normally. Release and proceed to Move 2.

a

8-MINUTE LOG				
exercise	move 1	move 2	move 3	move 4
sets				
reps				

MOVE 2: seated hand push
outer thighs and hips

a. Sit on a sturdy chair. Rest your feet on the floor with your knees bent at 90-degree angles. Place your palms on the outsides of your knees. While keeping your palms and arms stationary, push your knees outward against your palms, as if you were trying to push your palms away. At the same time, press inward with your hands, preventing your thighs from pushing them outward. Hold this isometric contraction for 1 minute, breathing normally. Release and proceed to Move 3 on page 214.

a

exercise sequence

1. warm up Jog or march in place for 1 minute.

2. cruise moves Do one 60-second repetition of each of your 4 Cruise Moves. Repeat this cycle and you will be done in 8 minutes.

3. cool down After your Cruise Moves, do these stretches (see page 194).

Sky-reaching pose | Hurdler's stretch | Cobra stretch

thighs day (cont'd)

MOVE 3: seated leg raise
fronts of the thighs

a. Sit on a sturdy chair. Rest your feet on the floor with your knees bent at 90-degree angles. Rest your hands on the chair at your sides. Exhale as you lift and extend your right leg. Hold for 30 seconds as you breathe normally. Then inhale as you lower your right leg and exhale as you repeat with your left leg. Hold for 30 seconds while breathing normally. Release and proceed to Move 4.

a

eat nutritionally, *not* emotionally®
visualization

Today you will again fill up your heart with love. You will expand on the visualization that you learned yesterday. Close your eyes and take a few deep, relaxing breaths, in through your nose and out through your mouth. Allow each exhalation to relax you more and more deeply. Once you feel completely relaxed, you are ready to begin.

MOVE 4: seated bridge
backs of the thighs and rear end

a. Sit on the edge of a sturdy chair. Rest your feet on the floor with your knees bent at 90-degree angles. Rest your palms on the chair at your sides. Exhale as you lift your hips, allowing your palms and feet to support your body weight. Continue to lift your hips until your body resembles the shape of a bridge. Hold for 20 to 60 seconds while breathing normally. Release and return to Move 1 on page 212. Repeat Moves 1–4 once more, and you're done.

a

extend your love

Imagine someone who loves you or has loved you very deeply. It may be the same person you imagined yesterday, or it may be someone new. Recall a specific instance when this person displayed unconditional love for you and allow your heart to be open to receiving this love—even if it wasn't open in real life. Feel your heart fill up and then overflow with gratitude and love.

Now, imagine that you are sending some love back to this loved one. Feel as if the two of you are joined by a continuously circulating current of loving feelings. See this person smile and glow with the warmth of the love you have shared. Feel good about yourself for sharing the love you have created with someone else.

Level 1
Thursday

"*They always say
time changes
things, but you
actually have to
change them
yourself.*"

—Andy Warhol

jorge's power thought

I've heard just about all of the excuses that were ever invented for not exercising or following a healthy diet. You know what? They are all lies. For example, here's one I hear all the time: People tell me that they don't have time to exercise. Not true. You need only 8 minutes a day. Who doesn't have 8 minutes?

Here's another one. I hear people make comments like, "Weight loss is not worth the effort. I'm just going to gain it back." You'll gain it back only if you stop practicing your new health habits. As long as you continue to stick to your Cruise Moves and Cruise Down Plate, any weight you lose will stay off.

Most of the lies that we tell ourselves stem from one giant lie. That lie is this: "I'm not good enough." When you believe you're not good enough, then you believe that you don't have the time to put into it. When you believe you're not good enough, you fail to make exercise and healthy eating a priority. The visualizations that you complete throughout your journey to lean hips and thin thighs will help you see that. For now, however, I want you to replace that lie with the truth. The truth is that **you _are_ worth it**. The truth is that your current body is the most precious gift you have ever been given.

"I know from my most successful clients that real weight loss happens only when your body becomes your highest priority."

8 minute moves®
torso and calves day

MOVE 1: stir hold
belly

a. Sit or stand with good posture. Lengthen
your spine and straighten your back. Relax
your shoulders. Exhale as you tighten your
abdominal muscles. Make a fist with one of
your hands and rub the bottom of your fist in a
circle over the center of your navel as if you
were stirring cake batter. This will force you to
keep your abs contracted strongly. Hold for
60 seconds as you breathe normally. Release
and proceed to Move 2.

a

8-MINUTE LOG				
exercise	move 1	move 2	move 3	move 4
sets				
reps				

MOVE 2: superman hold
lower back

a. Stand in front of a sturdy chair (one without wheels) with your left foot directly under your left hip. Bend forward and place your left palm on the chair seat, just under your left shoulder. Exhale as you raise and extend your right leg back and your right arm forward, forming a straight line from foot to fingertips. Hold for 30 seconds, release, and repeat on the other side. Then proceed to Move 3 on page 220.

a

exercise sequence

1. warm up Jog or march in place for 1 minute.

2. cruise moves Do one 60-second repetition of each of your 4 Cruise Moves. Repeat this cycle and you will be done in 8 minutes.

3. cool down After your Cruise Moves, do these stretches (see page 194).

Sky-reaching pose | Hurdler's stretch | Cobra stretch

torso and calves day (cont'd)

MOVE 3: airplane hold
shoulders

a. Sit or stand. Exhale and raise your arms out to your sides. Stop once your arms reach shoulder height. Keep your shoulders relaxed away from your ears. Hold firmly for 60 seconds, breathing normally, then proceed to Move 4

a

eat nutritionally, *not* emotionally®
visualization

Today you are going to use visualization to help build your inner gratitude. Once you build gratitude, you'll more easily be able to handle any negative emotions that may have led to overeating in the past. Close your eyes and take a few deep, relaxing breaths, in through your nose and out through your mouth. Every time you exhale, allow your body to grow more and more relaxed. Once you feel completely relaxed, you are ready to start.

MOVE 4: high heel hold
calves

a. Stand with your feet directly under your hips. Exhale as you lift your heels, rising onto the balls of your feet. Pretend you are wearing very high heels. (Place one hand on a chair or wall for balance, if needed.) Hold for 60 seconds, breathing normally. Release and return to Move 1 on page 218. Repeat Moves 1–4 once more, and you're done.

a

in praise of you

Reflect on your good qualities. First, start with what you do well. Are you a good friend or mother? Reflect on how you affect others in your life. What good things have you done in your life? Remember in every detail the good acts you've done. You might remember the birth of your child or a good deed you did for someone in need. Recall a time when you were instrumental in making someone else happy. Recall every detail of that memory. For the next few moments, continue to dwell on details in your past when you lived up to your expectations for yourself. Realize that you have done more good than bad in this world. Allow yourself to feel grateful for yourself. Allow this gratitude to grow in your heart.

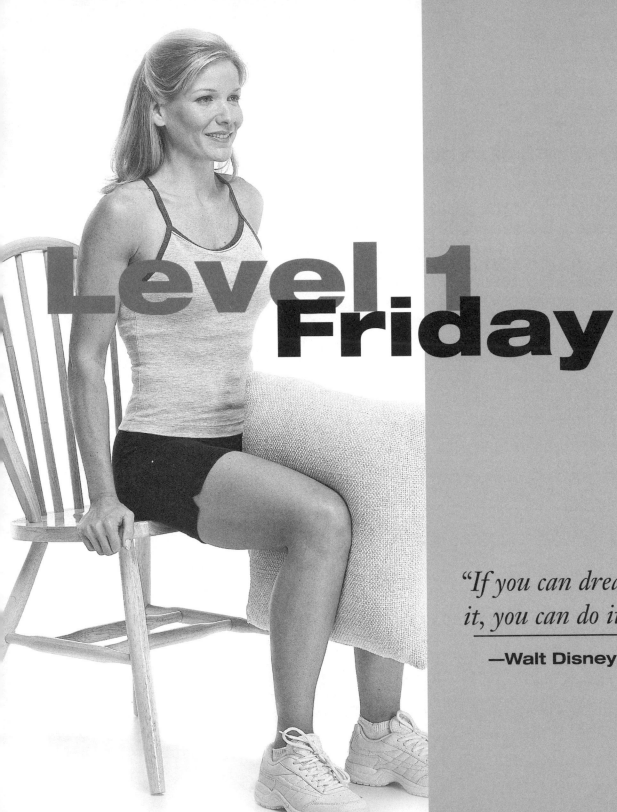

Level 1
Friday

"If you can dream it, you can do it."

—Walt Disney

jorge's power thought

Do you wish you could see what your future body will look like? Do you want to know what you will look like with leaner hips and thinner thighs? Some of my clients relied on photos of their youth—photos taken before they gained weight in their trouble zones—to help motivate them toward their goal. But I've found a better way. You can see your future body *today*, with the help of the World Wide Web.

As a member of JorgeCruise.com, you can see yourself in the future. This online tool will help you to create a photo of yourself at your future goal. It uses photo technology created by a company in Canada called MyVirtualModel. Simply follow the online directions and soon you'll see the future you—with leaner hips and thinner thighs. Then print out the photos and put them on your refrigerator to motivate you to stick with the program.

"Your photos of your future body will serve as a powerful motivating force. They will help keep you motivated and focused."

8 minute moves®
thighs day

MOVE 1: seated pillow squeeze
inner thighs

a. Sit on a sturdy chair (one without wheels). Rest your feet on the floor with your knees bent at 90-degree angles. Place a pillow between your thighs. Exhale as you squeeze the pillow between your thighs, as if you were trying to squeeze the stuffing out of the pillow. Hold for 1 minute as you breathe normally. Release and proceed to Move 2.

a

8-MINUTE LOG				
exercise	move 1	move 2	move 3	move 4
sets				
reps				

MOVE 2: seated hand push
outer thighs and hips

a. Sit on a sturdy chair. Rest your feet on the floor with your knees bent at 90-degree angles. Place your palms on the outsides of your knees. While keeping your palms and arms stationary, push your knees outward against your palms, as if you were trying to push your palms away. At the same time, press inward with your hands, preventing your thighs from pushing them outward. Hold this isometric contraction for 1 minute, breathing normally. Release and proceed to Move 3 on page 226.

a

exercise sequence

1. warm up Jog or march in place for 1 minute.

2. cruise moves Do one 60-second repetition of each of your 4 Cruise Moves. Repeat this cycle and you will be done in 8 minutes.

3. cool down After your Cruise Moves, do these stretches (see page 194).

Sky-reaching pose | Hurdler's stretch | Cobra stretch

thighs day (cont'd)

MOVE 3: seated leg raise
fronts of the thighs

a. Sit on a sturdy chair. Rest your feet on the floor with your knees bent at 90-degree angles. Rest your hands on the chair at your sides. Exhale as you lift and extend your right leg. Hold for 30 seconds as you breathe normally. Then inhale as you lower your right leg and exhale as you repeat with your left leg. Hold for 30 seconds while breathing normally. Release and proceed to Move 4.

a

eat nutritionally, *not* emotionally®
visualization

Today you are going to build so much love that your heart overflows, allowing you to share that love with others—even people you don't know that well! Once you fill up your own heart with love, it's so much easier to bring joy and peace to the lives of others. It's also so much easier to deal with difficult people who, in the past, may have caused you to plunge into a bad mood.

Start by taking a few deep, relaxing breaths, in through your nose and out through your mouth. Once you feel deeply relaxed, you're ready to begin.

MOVE 4: seated bridge
backs of the thighs and rear end

a. Sit on the edge of a sturdy chair. Rest your feet on the floor with your knees bent at 90-degree angles. Rest your palms on the chair at your sides. Exhale as you lift your hips, allowing your palms and feet to support your body weight. Continue to lift your hips until your body resembles the shape of a bridge. Hold for 20 to 60 seconds while breathing normally. Release and return to Move 1 on page 224. Repeat Moves 1–4 once more, and you're done.

a

overflowing love

Visualize a warm, white, loving energy growing in your heart. Feel this energy expand, filling up every space in your heart and making you feel content.

Visualize a person who needs help. It might be someone you know through church or someone who lives in your neighborhood or even in your house. Allow yourself to feel any pain or suffering that this person might be feeling.

Then, see the loving energy that you've created in your heart expand beyond your body and enter this person. See the energy fill their heart and wash away negativity. See the loving energy completely heal them of worry, mistrust, and anger. Feel good about yourself for helping someone else in need.

Level 1
Saturday

"It is never too late
to be what you
might have been."

—George Eliot

jorge's power thought

Today is your day off from Cruise Moves. Tomorrow you will also take the day off. Use this time to relax from your Cruise Moves.

Relaxation is just as important as exercise; it helps give your mind an important break. When you relax, you turn on your parasympathetic nervous system. This nervous system is the opposite of the one that governs your actions during the week. All too often we spend most of our time during the work week in a state of agitation, with our fight-or-flight response turned on. You must turn off your fight-or-flight response and turn on your parasympathetic nervous system from time to time. If you don't, your body and mind will become burned out. You'll feel irritable and fatigued. When you feel tired, you won't want to tackle your Cruise Moves.

I know some of you will feel guilty when you relax. You will think, "I know I should be doing something." When such guilty thoughts pop into your head, just use the "Oops" technique you learned earlier. Say "Oops" out loud and return to lounging in your hammock.

"Every good thing you do for your body—even relaxing—will help you reach your goal more quickly."

stretches
day off from cruise moves

Today is your day off from your Cruise Moves. To accelerate your results, I suggest that you spend 8 minutes this morning stretching and lengthening your muscles.

STRETCH 1: thigh lengthener
fronts of the thighs

a. Lie on your left side with your legs extended. Support your upper torso on your left forearm. Bend your right leg, grasping your foot with your right hand. Exhale as you use your hand to gently pull your right foot toward your buttocks as you simultaneously tuck in your tailbone and flatten the natural arch in your lower spine. Once in position, breathe normally as you hold the stretch for 30 seconds. Release and repeat on the other side. Then proceed to Stretch 2.

a

eat nutritionally, *not* emotionally®
visualization

During your last visualization, you shared your love with someone else. During this visualization, you will learn how to cultivate love toward those whom you experience difficulty getting along with. Close your eyes and take a few deep, relaxing breaths, in through your nose and out through your mouth. Allow each exhalation to bring you to a state of deep relaxation. Once you feel deeply relaxed, you're ready to begin.

STRETCH 2: seated forward bend
outer thighs and hips

a. Sit on the floor. Cross your legs so that your right foot rests in the crease made by your bent left knee and your right shin rests on top of your left shin, forming a triangle with your legs.

b. Inhale as you lengthen your spine. Exhale as you bend forward from the hips. Once in position, breathe normally, holding the stretch for 30 seconds. Then inhale as you rise to the starting position. Rearrange your legs so that your left shin is on top and repeat. Then proceed to Stretch 3 on page 232.

loving your enemies

See in your mind the image of a person with whom you experience difficulty getting along. Rather than focusing on this person's negative qualities, however, I want you to focus on what makes this person endearing. At first, this may be difficult, but visualize this person's good qualities and virtues. Perhaps this person is understanding or a good listener or a hard worker. Try to remember a time when you got along with this person. Perhaps she was kind to you during a time of stress. Cultivate this memory in your mind and try to call up every detail. As you do so, feel a sense of love growing in your heart. End your visualization by wishing that this person stay free from suffering. You'll be surprised by how much your positive wishes affect your relationship for the better!

stretches
day off from cruise moves (cont'd)

STRETCH 3: hamstring stretch
backs of the thighs

a. Lie on your back with your knees bent and feet on the floor. Lift your left leg, bringing your knee in toward your chest. Wrap a towel around the arch of your left foot, holding the ends of the towel in your hands.

b. Exhale as you extend your leg toward the ceiling. Use your hands to gently pull your foot toward your face. Breathe normally as you hold for 30 seconds. Lower your leg and repeat on the other side. Then proceed to Stretch 4.

STRETCH 4: frog
inner thighs

a. Start in a table position with your knees under your hips and hands under your shoulders. Widen your knees 6 to 12 inches and turn your toes outward.

b. Exhale as you gently bring your hips back toward your feet, feeling a stretch in your inner thighs and groin. Once in position, hold for 60 seconds as you breathe normally. Then release and return to Stretch 1 on page 230. Repeat Stretches 1–4 once more, and you're done.

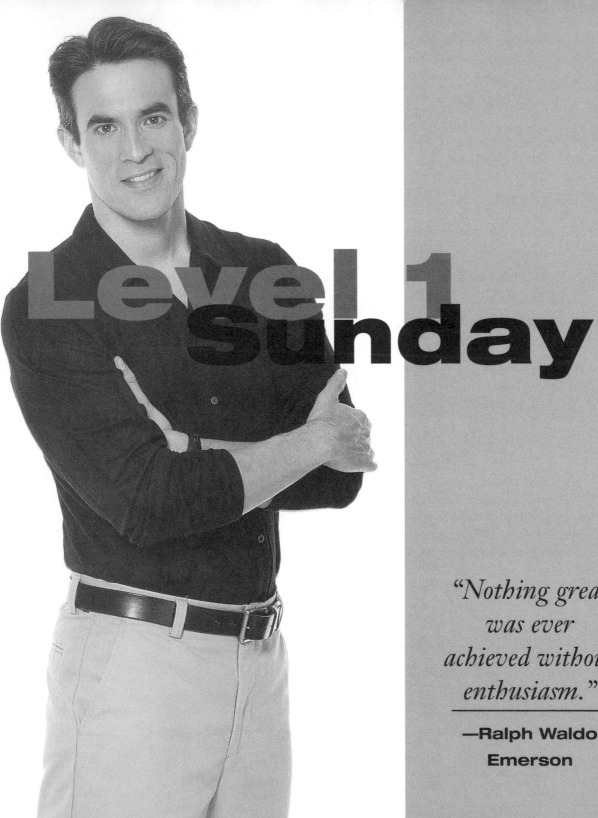

Level 1
Sunday

"Nothing great
was ever
achieved without
enthusiasm."

—Ralph Waldo
Emerson

jorge's power thought

Today is your day off from your Cruise Moves. I encourage you to spend the extra 8 minutes today preparing for the week to come. Flip through cookbooks or your recipe collection and pick some meals for the week. Then create your shopping list.

Write down the meals you plan to eat during the week, particularly lunch and dinner. Pencil these meals into your day planner, along with the time that you plan to eat them. If you need to do anything to make sure that meal happens—like running to the grocery store—pencil in that task as well.

You also might spend more time in the kitchen by chopping up some veggies to eat during the week. Or you might cook up a bunch of food during the day and create your own homemade frozen dinners. Use Sunday as your planning day. It will help you to stay on track.

"Follow the Boy Scout motto and be prepared. A little extra preparation on Sundays can make the rest of your week flow so much more easily."

capture your progress
day off from cruise moves

Today is your day off. Take a moment to relish your progress. Grab a pen and answer the following questions. Then share the answers with me by sending an e-mail to thinthigh1@jorgecruise.com.

1. What is your current weight?

_____

2. What was your original weight?

_____

3. What is your waist circumference in inches?

_____

4. What was your original waist circumference in inches?

_____

5. What have you done well this week? What are you most proud of?

_____

_____

_____

_____

_____

6. What could you improve next week?

_____

_____

_____

_____

_____

_____

eat nutritionally, *not* emotionally®
visualization

One of the first steps to eliminating emotional eating begins with you. It begins will treating yourself with the utmost respect, and you can do that only if you love yourself and your body. Sometimes cultivating self-love in the place of self-hate can be difficult. Today, you will complete a visualization that will help. Close your eyes and take a few deep, relaxing breaths, in through your nose and out through your mouth. Allow each exhalation to bring you to a state of deep relaxation. Once you feel completely relaxed, you're ready to begin.

cheryl mccowan shrunk 3½ inches off her thighs!

"The best part of the Jorge Cruise® program is the minimal amount of time involved. It fits perfectly into my morning routine. I am able to get up from bed, get on the floor, and, before I realize that I am actually exercising, it's over! And I still get the benefits. For the amount of time involved—8 minutes—you have to be just plain lazy not to try it.

"My results have inspired me to move even more. I am more active overall and I feel that I want to be outdoors doing things like walking and riding my bike. I have more energy and don't find myself sitting around as much. I've truly changed my lifestyle for the better."

Cheryl slimmed down her thighs and lost 13 pounds.

cultivating inner love

Think back to a time in your life when you felt good about yourself. Perhaps you accomplished something significant, won an award, or got a promotion at work. Whatever it was, bring the memory of that happy time fully into your awareness.

See every detail of that moment. Try to feel the emotions that you felt during that happy time. Think back to the smells, sights, sounds, and sensations of that moment. Try to recall it as vividly as possible. Take a few moments to relish

the good feeling that you've just created inside of yourself. Know that these positive feelings are always there inside of you, waiting to be called upon at any moment.

Level 2
Monday

> "There came a time when the risk to remain tight in a bud was more painful than the risk it took to blossom."
>
> —Anaïs Nin

jorge's power thought

Many people ask me why I suggest you perform each Cruise Move for 60 seconds. Besides the fact that it allows your Cruise Move session to total a nice and neat 8 minutes, I do have some other, more important reasons. I didn't pick 60 seconds out of thin air!

Some resistance-training programs require you to count repetitions, suggesting that you lift a weight 12 to 15 times. My first book did this. I've found in working with millions of clients that simply watching the clock is sometimes an easier way to move! It frees your mind from counting and forces you to fully fatigue the muscle you are working. It's super simple and convenient.

But why 60 seconds? I've found with much trial and error that 60 seconds is the ideal amount of time needed to start firming your muscles. In testing my Jorge Cruise® programs on client after client, they loved it and saw the results!

"I learned my most important lessons about weight loss from people just like you."

8 minute moves®
thighs day

MOVE 1: standing leg swing
inner thighs

a. Stand next to a chair or wall, placing your left hand on the chair or wall for support. Your feet should be directly under your hips. Shift your body weight over your left foot. Inhale as you lift your right foot off the floor and outward slightly.

b. Exhale as you swing your right foot to the left, in front of and past your left leg. Hold for a count of 2. Inhale as you return to the starting position. Repeat for 30 seconds. Switch legs and repeat for 30 seconds, then proceed to Move 2.

a

b

8-MINUTE LOG				
exercise	move 1	move 2	move 3	move 4
sets				
reps				

MOVE 2: standing side raise
outer thighs and hips

a. Stand next to a chair or wall, placing your left hand on the chair or wall for support. Your feet should be directly under your hips. Shift your body weight over your left foot. Exhale as you lift and extend your right leg laterally away from your torso as far as you can. Hold for a count of 2. Inhale as you return to the starting position. Repeat for 30 seconds. Switch legs and repeat for 30 seconds, then proceed to Move 3 on page 242.

a

exercise sequence

1. warm up Jog or march in place for 1 minute.

2. cruise moves Do one 60-second repetition of each of your 4 Cruise Moves. Repeat this cycle and you will be done in 8 minutes.

3. cool down After your Cruise Moves, do these stretches (see page 194).

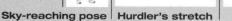

Sky-reaching pose | **Hurdler's stretch** | **Cobra stretch**

thighs day (cont'd)

MOVE 3: standing knee lift
fronts of the thighs

a. Stand next to a chair or wall, placing your right hand on the chair or wall for support. Your feet should be directly under your hips. Shift your body weight over your right foot. Exhale as you lift your left knee, until your left thigh is parallel with the floor. Hold for a count of 2. Inhale and release. Repeat for 30 seconds. Switch legs, repeat for 30 seconds, and then proceed to Move 4.

a

eat nutritionally, *not* emotionally®
visualization

For today's visualization, I'd like you to explore your own passion and see where it will take you. You'll find that you can use your passion as a powerful motivating force. It will help you stick with your new health habits. Close your eyes and take a few deep, relaxing breaths, in through your nose and out through your mouth. Allow each exhalation to bring you to a state of deep relaxation. Once you feel completely relaxed, you're ready to begin.

MOVE 4: standing leg lift
backs of the thighs and rear end

a. Stand facing a chair or wall. Place one or both hands against the chair or wall for support. Shift your body weight over your left foot. Exhale as you lift and extend your right leg behind your torso as high as you can. Be careful not to overarch your lower back as you do so. Hold for a count of 2. Inhale and release. Repeat for 30 seconds. Switch legs, repeat, and then return to Move 1 on page 240. Repeat Moves 1–4 once more, and you're done.

a

unleash your inner passion

Visualize yourself 1 year in the future. See yourself as you would like to be. You are accomplishing all of the things that you wanted in life with strength and vigor. You are focusing on what's most important to you and making your mark on the world.

What new mental, physical, and spiritual qualities have you uncovered? What lessons have you learned? What did you develop inside of yourself to be able to accomplish so much? What was most important in helping you to achieve success? What helped you overcome any challenges along the way?

With those answers, return to the present moment and visualize what you must do right now to make your future become reality.

Level 2
Tuesday

"*The great dividing line between success and failure can be expressed in five words, 'I did not have time.'*"

—Franklin Field

jorge's power thought

As you progress along your journey to lean hips and thin thighs, it may help to revisit the reason you started this journey in the first place. Have you ever known someone who was so passionate and so focused that nothing could stand in his or her way? Usually such passion comes from having a very clear plan—a mental blueprint—that guides you successfully toward your goal.

To ignite your passion for leaner hips and thinner thighs, take a moment to think about what you want your new, dream body to look like. You might even take out a piece of paper and jot down some notes. Write down not only how you want your hips and thighs to look, but also how you want them to feel. Also write down what you'd like others to notice about your hips and thighs. And even write down what types of clothes you might wear or feel more comfortably wearing once you reach your dream goal.

Whenever you feel like you need an extra bit of motivation, you can turn to the list you just created to remind yourself *why* you decided to take this journey. Remember: It's well worth the effort.

> "With a clear target, you have the most powerful advantage to making your dream body a reality."

8 minute moves®
upper-body day

MOVE 1: wall pump
chest

a. Stand arm's length away from a wall with your feet directly under your hips. Lean forward and place your palms against the wall. Your elbows should be slightly bent.

b. Inhale as you slowly bend your elbows, bringing your chest and torso closer to the wall. Exhale as you slowly press yourself back to the starting position, straightening your arms as you go. Slowly repeat for 60 seconds. Release and proceed to Move 2.

a

b

8-MINUTE LOG				
exercise	move 1	move 2	move 3	move 4
sets				
reps				

MOVE 2: posture pump
upper back

a. Stand with your heels, buttocks, and head against a wall or sturdy, closed door. Rest your arms comfortably at your sides.

b. Exhale as you pull your upper back and shoulders toward the wall, flattening everything from your ribs to your shoulders against the wall. Get your lower back as close as possible to the wall as you can. Relax and repeat for 60 seconds. Proceed to Move 3 on page 248.

a

b

exercise sequence

1. warm up Jog or march in place for 1 minute.

2. cruise moves Do one 60-second repetition of each of your 4 Cruise Moves. Repeat this cycle and you will be done in 8 minutes.

3. cool down After your Cruise Moves, do these stretches (see page 194).

Sky-reaching pose | **Hurdler's stretch** | **Cobra stretch**

upper-body day (cont'd)

MOVE 3: book hold
biceps

a. Stand with your feet directly under your hips. Balance a heavy textbook or phone book in each hand with your palms facing up and your arms bent at 90 degrees. Hold for 60 seconds as you breathe normally, keeping your back long and straight and your abdominals firm. Release and proceed to Move 4.

a

eat nutritionally, *not* emotionally®
visualization

Visualization can help you to face life's little challenges with more ease. Instead of problems, you see solutions. Instead of turning to food, you can turn to your mind for help. When life throws you a lemon, you can easily turn it into lemonade! Let's use visualization to help you turn your first lemon into *lemonaid*, shall we? Close your eyes and take a few deep, relaxing breaths, in through your nose and out through your mouth. Allow each exhalation to bring you to a state of deep relaxation. Once you feel completely relaxed, you're ready to begin.

MOVE 4: kickback hold
triceps

a. Stand with your feet directly under your hips. Bend forward from your hips about 45 degrees with your arms extended.

b. Exhale as you lift your extended arms up behind your torso. Stop once you've lifted your arms as high as possible without locking your elbows. Hold for 60 seconds, breathing normally. Release and return to Move 1 on page 246. Repeat Moves 1–4 once more, and you're done.

a

b

mental lemonade

You're driving home when suddenly, you hear a "clunk, clunk, clunk" sound as your car begins to bounce around. It's a flat tire! Instead of panicking, you calmly steer your car to the side of the road and turn on your hazard lights. Carefully you open your door and get out to assess the situation and then go to your trunk and retrieve the spare tire, car jack, and lug wrench. See yourself removing the hubcap, loosening the lug nuts, and positioning the jack. You use strong, solid, even strokes on the jack and up your car goes! You remove the flat tire and hoist it back in your trunk, install the spare, replace the lug nuts, lower your car, replace the hubcap, and go on your way. How do you feel knowing that you can overcome any obstacle that comes your way?

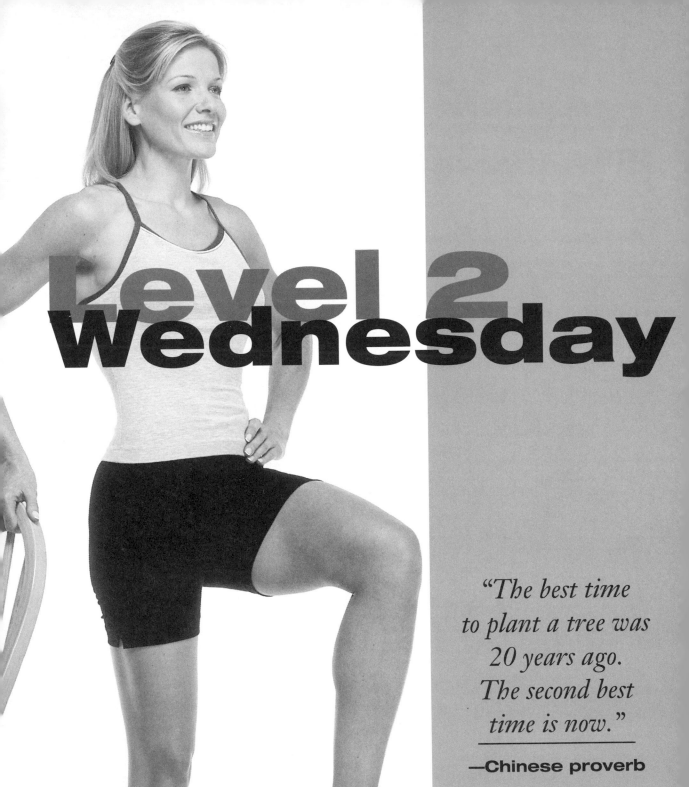

Level 2
Wednesday

*"The best time
to plant a tree was
20 years ago.
The second best
time is now."*

—Chinese proverb

jorge's power thought

All of us have what I like to call a loser zone, a place where we spend too much of our time. You fall into a loser zone when you do something that produces no significant improvement in your life. The number one loser zone activity? Watching television. When you watch TV, you're not only sedentary—and therefore burning very few calories—but you are also more likely to eat mindlessly. Commercials that depict food will make you crave food when you are not truly hungry.

Other loser zones include aimlessly chatting on the phone and surfing the Internet. What are your loser zones and how many hours a day do you spend losing precious time? I'm not suggesting that you should be on the go all the time. As I've said before, relaxation is very important. However, if you spend more than 6 to 8 hours a week in loser zone activities, you have just found some time that could be better spent focusing on your hips and thighs!

"Shrink your loser zones and you'll maximize the time you have to spend fighting your trouble zones."

8 minute moves®
thighs day

MOVE 1: standing leg swing
inner thighs

a. Stand next to a chair or wall, placing your left hand on the chair or wall for support. Your feet should be directly under your hips. Shift your body weight over your left foot. Inhale as you lift your right foot off the floor and outward slightly.

b. Exhale as you swing your right foot to the left, in front of and past your left leg. Hold for a count of 2. Inhale as you return to the starting position. Repeat for 30 seconds. Switch legs and repeat for 30 seconds, then proceed to Move 2.

a

b

8-MINUTE LOG				
exercise	move 1	move 2	move 3	move 4
sets				
reps				

MOVE 2: standing side raise
outer thighs and hips

a. Stand next to a chair or wall, placing your left hand on the chair or wall for support. Your feet should be directly under your hips. Shift your body weight over your left foot. Exhale as you lift and extend your right leg laterally away from your torso as far as you can. Hold for a count of 2. Inhale as you return to the starting position. Repeat for 30 seconds. Switch legs and repeat for 30 seconds, then proceed to Move 3 on page 254.

a

exercise sequence

1. warm up Jog or march in place for 1 minute.

2. cruise moves Do one 60-second repetition of each of your 4 Cruise Moves. Repeat this cycle and you will be done in 8 minutes.

3. cool down After your Cruise Moves, do these stretches (see page 194).

Sky-reaching pose | **Hurdler's stretch** | **Cobra stretch**

thighs day (cont'd)

MOVE 3: standing knee lift
fronts of the thighs

a. Stand next to a chair or wall, placing your right hand on the chair or wall for support. Your feet should be directly under your hips. Shift your body weight over your right foot. Exhale as you lift your left knee, until your left thigh is parallel with the floor. Hold for a count of 2. Inhale and release. Repeat for 30 seconds. Switch legs, repeat for 30 seconds, and then proceed to Move 4.

a

eat nutritionally, *not* emotionally®
visualization

For today's visualization, you will again use the power of your mind to help you solve problems that might have led to emotional eating in the past. Today you will use visualization to help you overcome the urge to eat when you encounter difficult

people. Take a few moments to relax by taking a few deep breaths, in through your nose and out through your mouth. Feel each exhalation relax you more and more deeply. Once you are fully relaxed, you are ready to begin.

MOVE 4: standing leg lift
backs of the thighs and rear end

a. Stand facing a chair or wall. Place one or both hands against the chair or wall for support. Shift your body weight over your left foot. Exhale as you lift and extend your right leg behind your torso as high as you can. Be careful not to overarch your lower back as you do so. Hold for a count of 2. Inhale and release. Repeat for 30 seconds. Switch legs, repeat, and then return to Move 1 on page 252. Repeat Moves 1–4 once more, and you're done.

a

seeing your problems vanish

Imagine someone with whom you may be having some personal conflict. It might be your spouse or your child or someone at work. Bring the image of that person into your mind. Imagine having a positive interaction with that person. Start with some small talk. See yourself confronting this person about what is bothering you. See yourself calmly, nicely, and succinctly voicing your concerns, keeping the focus on how this person makes you feel. See this person respond positively. You will soon find that if you mentally see yourself confronting your problems, you won't feel so much stress or anxiety when you try to solve them in real life!

Level 2
Thursday

"Inaction saps the vigor of the mind."

—Leonardo da Vinci

jorge's power thought

Many people ask me for secrets on getting out of bed in the morning. They tell me that they are not a morning person, and that they just can't exercise as soon as they jump out of bed.

I always share this simple trick. To help jump start your morning, do the following as soon as the alarm goes off. Sit up in bed and bring your hands together for a strong clap. With every breath, clap strongly. The palms of your hands have more nerve receptors than almost any other part of your body. Clapping your hands creates a neurological jolt that literally stimulates your brain. Then jump out of bed and stand up with good posture. Bring your shoulders back and your chest out. This will activate your diaphragm muscle (located under your lungs), which helps maximize your oxygen intake. Then jog in place. That will get your heart pumping.

Trust me on this one. If you do that simple technique, you'll be out of bed and ready for your Cruise Moves in no time.

"An extra hour of sleep will help to reset your body clock, allowing you to wake up refreshed."

8 minute moves®
torso and calves day

MOVE 1: belly breath pump
belly

a. Stand with your feet directly under your hips. As you exhale, contract and press your tummy muscles inward as you slowly squeeze all the breath out of your lungs.

b. Reverse the motion by relaxing your tummy outward to slowly pull air into your lungs. Repeat for 1 minute, fully emptying and filling your lungs. Then proceed to Move 2.

a

b

8-MINUTE LOG				
exercise	move 1	move 2	move 3	move 4
sets				
reps				

MOVE 2: superman
lower back

a. Lie with your belly on the floor, your legs straight, and your arms extended in front of you, like Superman flying through the air. Exhale as you simultaneously lift your arms and legs about 4 inches off the floor. If you begin to feel pinching in your lower back, focus on length-ening your spine by reaching out through your fingertips and toes. Also, make sure your head remains in a neutral position with your gaze at the floor. Hold for 1 minute and then proceed to Move 3 on page 260.

a

exercise sequence

1. warm up Jog or march in place for 1 minute.

2. cruise moves Do one 60-second repetition of each of your 4 Cruise Moves. Repeat this cycle and you will be done in 8 minutes.

3. cool down After your Cruise Moves, do these stretches (see page 194).

Sky-reaching pose | **Hurdler's stretch** | **Cobra stretch**

torso and calves day (cont'd)

MOVE 3: bird pump
shoulders

a. Stand with your feet directly under your hips and your arms resting at your sides. Raise and extend your arms about 45 degrees out from your hips. Make sure your shoulders are relaxed, your tummy is firm, and your upper back straight.

b. Exhale as you raise your arms about 45 degrees above shoulder level. Inhale as you lower them to the starting position. Slowly repeat for 1 minute. Release and proceed to Move 4.

a

b

eat nutritionally, *not* emotionally® visualization

Many of my clients tell me that they are most likely to overeat when they feel worthless or "not good enough." Today's visualization will help you to overcome such feelings. Today you will cultivate your inner self-love. Close your eyes and take a few deep, relaxing breaths, in through your nose and out through your mouth. Once you feel completely relaxed, you are ready to begin.

MOVE 4: standing calf pump
calves

a. Stand next to a sturdy chair or wall with your feet directly under your hips and your arms resting at your sides. Place one hand on the chair or wall for balance.

b. Exhale as you rise onto the balls of your feet, bringing your heels off the floor. Inhale as you lower your heels back to the floor. Repeat for 1 minute, then return to Move 1 on page 258. Repeat Moves 1–4 once more, and you're done.

a

b

you at center stage

See yourself through the eyes of someone else, someone who really cares about you, such as a close friend, a spouse, or one of your children. Feel the same admiration that this person feels as you watch yourself through their eyes. Try to see all of the good qualities about yourself that *they* see every day.

Watch yourself as your loved ones walk up to you

and tell you how much they love and admire you. Watch your expression as they tell you about your good qualities. What do they say? Now imagine more and more people coming into the room and staring at you with the same love and admiration of your loved one. As the room fills with people, they begin to applaud, clapping for you!

Level 2
Friday

"You should plant your own garden instead of waiting for someone else to bring you flowers."

—Veronica Shoffstall

jorge's power thought

Many people ask me whether they can skip their cooldown. They tell me that stretching won't help them create leaner hips and thinner thighs, so why bother? Well, that's simply not true.

Stretching helps you accomplish your goal in a number of ways. Most important, stretching helps increase *flexibility*, which in turn, helps your muscles to grow stronger. Yes, it's true! Researchers have found that flexible muscles tend to be stronger and more aerobic than tight muscles. Also, stretching will help to **lengthen your muscles,** creating a long, lean appearance. Finally, it helps to bring circulation to your muscles, allowing them to more quickly recover from your Cruise Moves. This circulation is also important in preventing cellulite. So keep stretching!

"Your cooldown will help prepare your body to face the day, allowing you to feel refreshed."

8 minute moves®
thighs day

MOVE 1: standing leg swing
inner thighs

a. Stand next to a chair or wall, placing your left hand on the chair or wall for support. Your feet should be directly under your hips. Shift your body weight over your left foot. Inhale as you lift your right foot off the floor and outward slightly.

b. Exhale as you swing your right foot to the left, in front of and past your left leg. Hold for a count of 2. Inhale as you return to the starting position. Repeat for 30 seconds. Switch legs and repeat for 30 seconds, then proceed to Move 2.

a

b

8-MINUTE LOG				
exercise	move 1	move 2	move 3	move 4
sets				
reps				

MOVE 2: standing side raise
outer thighs and hips

a. Stand next to a chair or wall, placing your left hand on the chair or wall for support. Your feet should be directly under your hips. Shift your body weight over your left foot. Exhale as you lift and extend your right leg laterally away from your torso as far as you can. Hold for a count of 2. Inhale as you return to the starting position. Repeat for 30 seconds. Switch legs and repeat for 30 seconds, then proceed to Move 3 on page 266.

a

exercise sequence

1. warm up Jog or march in place for 1 minute.

2. cruise moves Do one 60-second repetition of each of your 4 Cruise Moves. Repeat this cycle and you will be done in 8 minutes.

3. cool down After your Cruise Moves, do these stretches (see page 194).

Sky-reaching pose | **Hurdler's stretch** | **Cobra stretch**

thighs day (cont'd)

MOVE 3: standing knee lift
fronts of the thighs

a. Stand next to a chair or wall, placing your right hand on the chair or wall for support. Your feet should be directly under your hips. Shift your body weight over your right foot. Exhale as you lift your left knee, until your left thigh is parallel with the floor. Hold for a count of 2. Inhale and release. Repeat for 30 seconds. Switch legs, repeat for 30 seconds, and then proceed to Move 4.

a

eat nutritionally, *not* emotionally®
visualization

Today you will again use the power of visualization to help you to better deal the emotions that may arise from encounters with difficult people. Close your eyes and take a few deep, relaxing breaths, in through your nose and out through your mouth. Allow each exhalation to relax you more deeply. Once you feel completely relaxed, you are ready to begin.

MOVE 4: standing leg lift
backs of the thighs and rear end

a. Stand facing a chair or wall. Place one or both hands against the chair or wall for support. Shift your body weight over your left foot. Exhale as you lift and extend your right leg behind your torso as high as you can. Be careful not to overarch your lower back as you do so. Hold for a count of 2. Inhale and release. Repeat for 30 seconds. Switch legs, repeat, and then return to Move 1 on page 264. Repeat Moves 1–4 once more, and you're done.

a

dealing with difficult people

Someone who makes you feel a negative emotion almost as soon as you imagine his or her face. If the image of this person makes you feel very angry, sad, or anxious, take a few deep, relaxing breaths to help yourself return to a more relaxed state. Then, put yourself in this person's shoes. Try to imagine what a typical day in this person's life must be like. Experience every encounter and every emotion. Imagine how you would feel if you lived the same life as this person. Imagine how you would like others to respond to you.

After you are done, notice whether you have any new insights into this person. Notice whether the image of this person evokes the same strong emotions as it did before the visualization.

Level 2
Saturday

"*Some people wait so long for their ship to come in, their pier collapses.*"

—John Goddard

jorge's power thought

I've already told you that you must get enough sleep to allow your muscles to repair themselves. Did you know that a solid night's sleep can also sharpen your mind and lift your spirits? That's right, simply getting enough Zzz's helps make concentration easier, and even improves your ability to learn. This is because the more sleep you get, the more minutes your brain spends in the rapid eye movement (REM) phase of sleep. And REM sleep is crucial for cementing new information into long- and short-term memory. Research suggests that it is during REM sleep that we file away everything we learn.

Getting enough sleep is as important to your overall health as regular exercise and a healthy diet. Sometimes my clients tell me that they have trouble falling asleep at night. They say worrisome thoughts keep them awake. I tell them to try this little trick. Lie on your back and breathe deeply 10 times. Then lie on your right side and breathe deeply 15 times. Then lie on your left side and breathe deeply 20 times . . . if you don't fall asleep before then, that is!

"Try taking a warm bath before bed to soothe away stressful thoughts or tension that might be keeping you awake."

stretches
day off from cruise moves

Today is your day off from your Cruise Moves. To accelerate your results, I suggest that you spend 8 minutes this morning stretching and lengthening your muscles.

STRETCH 1: butt kick
fronts of the thighs

a. Lie on your belly with your legs extended. Bend your left arm and rest your head in the crook created by your arm. Bend your right leg, bringing your right foot toward your buttocks. Reach back with your right hand and grasp your right foot. Exhale as you use your right hand to gently pull your right foot toward your buttocks. Inhale, and, then, to deepen the stretch, exhale as you press your pubic bone downward into the floor, flattening the natural arch in your lower spine. Hold for a few breaths and then release the pelvic tilt and repeat, holding and releasing over and over for 30 seconds. Release and repeat with the other leg, then proceed to Stretch 2.

a

eat nutritionally, *not* emotionally®
visualization

Today you will use the power of visualization to help overcome negative feelings that can lead to overeating. You can use this visualization any time you feel a negative mood coming on. Use it whenever you find a negative emotion causing you to think of food.

Start by relaxing with a few deep breaths, in through your nose and out through your mouth. Once you feel deeply relaxed, you are ready to begin.

STRETCH 2: standing hip opener
outer thighs and hips

a. Stand facing a sturdy table. Lift your left thigh in toward your chest, placing your left foot on the tabletop. Turn out your left knee so that your left shin forms a parallel line with the edge of the table. Place your palms on the table for balance.

b. To increase the stretch, lean forward from your hips. Hold for 30 seconds, breathing normally. Switch legs and repeat, then proceed to Stretch 3 on page 272.

replacing bad with good

Notice the state of your mind. Are you feeling any negative emotions? Do you feel angry, sad, depressed, anxious, or fearful? Each time you exhale, see yourself releasing these negative feelings out of your body. See your breath literally blow them away! Then, each time you inhale, visualize yourself breathing in positive emotions such as love, compassion, joy, and peace. With each breath, exchange a negative emotion for a positive one, and feel your body begin to vibrate with positive emotions!

stretches
day off from cruise moves (cont'd)

STRETCH 3: forward bend
backs of the thighs

a. Stand with your back and buttocks against a wall and your feet about a foot in front of the wall. Exhale as you lean forward from the hips, allowing the wall to support your buttocks. Interlace your forearms and relax your upper body. Hold for 60 seconds as you breathe normally. Release and proceed to Stretch 4.

a

STRETCH 4: wide-angle forward bend
inner thighs

a. Stand with your feet about 3 feet apart. Inhale as you reach your arms overhead. Exhale as you bend forward from your hips, reaching through your fingertips as you bend forward. Try to keep your abs firm and back flat as you bend. Interlace your forearms and relax your upper body. Hold for 60 seconds as you breathe normally. Release and return to Stretch 1 on page 270. Repeat Stretches 1–4 once more, and you're done.

a

Level 2
Sunday

"The greatest discovery of my time is that human beings can alter their lives by altering their attitudes."

—William James

jorge's power thought

Following the Cruise Down Plate will do more than help you avoid overeating. It will also help you eat more fruits and vegetables, many of which are loaded with vitamin C, which plays a very important role in muscle recovery after your Cruise Moves.

This important vitamin helps produce collagen, which is a connective tissue that holds muscles, bones, and other tissues together. During exercise, as the rate of your breathing increases to meet the demands of your workout, the chemical interaction of oxygen with your cell membranes, protein, and other cellular components creates damaging substances called free radicals. These free radicals are highly reactive substances that, much like small fires, must be extinguished before they burn, or "oxidize" neighboring molecules in other cells, creating muscle soreness and stiffness.

Vitamin C is a dietary antioxidant that helps to put out free radical damage in and around your cells. So follow up your Cruise Moves with a breakfast rich in vitamin C foods such as oranges, red peppers, or cantaloupe.

"Brightly colored fruits and vegetables such as red peppers are packed with vitamin C."

capture your progress
day off from cruise moves

Today is your day off. Take a moment to relish your progress. Grab a pen and answer the following questions. Then share the answers with me by sending an e-mail to thinthighs2@jorgecruise.com.

1. What is your current weight?

_____

2. What was your original weight?

_____

3. What is your waist circumference in inches?

_____

4. What was your original waist circumference in inches?

_____

5. What have you done well this week? What are you most proud of?

_____

_____

_____

_____

_____

6. What could you improve next week?

_____

_____

_____

_____

_____

eat nutritionally, *not* emotionally®
visualization

Today you will use the power of visualization to help fill yourself up with positive emotions. This visualization is similar to the one you learned on Saturday. You may find that one works better for you than the other. Use whichever one works best for you to help transform bad moods into good ones.

Start by taking a few deep, relaxing breaths, in through your nose and out through your mouth. Allow each exhalation to relax you more deeply. Once you feel completely relaxed, you are ready to begin.

Eleanor Talbot lost 13½ inches!

"The 60 pounds I've lost are exciting, but knowing that I have lost 6½ inches from one thigh and 7 inches from the other is totally amazing.

"These thigh moves are so easy to do. They take only minutes to complete three times weekly, and they are totally effective! I can really 'feel the burn.' The exercises don't take much longer than the original *8 Minutes in the Morning*, but are totally targeted to work the entire thigh.

"The People Solution has been KEY to my success, too! Communication with my friends (by e-mail, on the phone, at JorgeCruise.com, or in person) is what I *really* need, not food! "One other thing. . . . When I was a kid, one of the 'nicknames' I was called was 'Thunder Thighs.' NOW, I'm working to have THINNER THIGHS!"

Eleanor lost 13½ inches! Eleanor was also featured on Dateline NBC's Ultimate Diet Challenge, where the Jorge Cruise® Plan was compared to five other leading national programs. She ended up losing more weight than those on SlimFast® and Weight Watchers®. Congratulations, Eleanor!

seeing yourself clearly

Visualize yourself, standing in front of you. See your face and body. See your outfit and hairstyle. Notice how the person—you—standing in front of you feels right now. Become aware of any negative feelings—stress, anger, depression, and so on. Feel love and compassion toward the "you" in front of you, just as you would feel toward a child experiencing these same negative feelings. Allow the love you have stored up in your heart to expand and grow and fill up the "you" standing in front of you. See yourself become filled with compassionate, loving energy. Seeing yourself comforting and hugging the "you" that you see in front of you. See yourself smile.

Level 3
Monday

jorge's power thought

You need protein to help build lean muscle, and fish is one of the best protein sources around. Besides quality protein, certain types of cold-water fatty fish contain a special type of fat called omega-3 fatty acids. These special fats have been shown to help reduce muscle soreness after a workout. They also help to boost your mood, turn down your appetite, and give your skin a radiant glow.

What type of fish should you eat? I recommend you stick with salmon. This type of fish is very rich in omega-3 fatty acids. And according to the Environmental Protection Agency, it's the type of fish that is least likely to contain contaminants such as PCBs and mercury, making it safe for pregnant and nursing women. Low mercury levels are particularly important because mercury poisoning leads to fatigue and headaches. When you feel tired and have a headache, you'll be less likely to complete your Cruise Moves. So stick with salmon and enjoy the goodness of fish without the pollutants.

"The fatty acids in cold-water fish such as salmon are important for helping your muscles recover from your Cruise Moves."

8 minute moves®
thighs day

MOVE 1: reclined pillow squeeze
inner thighs

a. Lie on your back with your knees bent and your feet on the floor. Place a thick, firm pillow between your thighs.

b. Exhale as you lift your hips, balancing your body weight on your upper back and feet. Squeeze the pillow between your thighs as if you were trying to squeeze the stuffing out of it. Hold for 40 to 60 seconds as you breathe normally. Release and proceed to Move 2.

a

b

8-MINUTE LOG				
exercise	move 1	move 2	move 3	move 4
sets				
reps				

MOVE 2: doggie hold
outer thighs and hips

a. Kneel on your hands and knees. Make sure your hands are under your shoulders and your knees are under your hips.

b. Keeping your leg bent at a 90-degree angle, exhale as you lift your right leg out to the side (like a dog at a fire hydrant). Hold for 30 seconds. Lower and repeat with the other leg, then proceed to Move 3 on page 282.

a

b

exercise sequence

1. warm up Jog or march in place for 1 minute.

2. cruise moves Do one 60-second repetition of each of your 4 Cruise Moves. Repeat this cycle and you will be done in 8 minutes.

3. cool down After your Cruise Moves, do these stretches (see page 194).

Sky-reaching pose | **Hurdler's stretch** | **Cobra stretch**

thighs day (cont'd)

MOVE 3: seated leg lift
fronts of the thighs

a. Sit on the floor with your left leg bent and your right leg extended. Wrap your hands around your left knee for support. Sit with your back long and straight. Try not to slouch.

b. Exhale as you lift your extended right leg as high as you can. Hold for 30 seconds while you breathe normally. Lower and repeat with the other leg, then proceed to Move 4.

a

b

eat nutritionally, *not* emotionally®
visualization

Today you will use the power of your mind-body connection to fuel your motivation stick to your Cruise Down Plate. During today's visualization, you will imagine a whole day's worth of your favorite healthy food choices. So close your eyes and take a few deep, relaxing breaths, in through your nose and out through your mouth. Allow each exhalation to bring you to a state of deep relaxation. Once you feel completely relaxed, you're ready to begin.

MOVE 4: kneeling leg lift
backs of the thighs and rear end

a. Kneel on the floor with your hands under your shoulders and your knees under your hips.

b. Exhale as you extend and lift your right leg slightly higher than your torso. Hold for 30 seconds. Release and repeat with your left leg, then return to Move 1 on page 280. Repeat Moves 1–4 once more, and you're done.

a

b

seeing healthy foods

You're heading to the kitchen to prepare yourself a wholesome breakfast. Will you be filling your Cruise Down Plate with scrambled egg whites, a piece of whole-grain toast with a little butter, and an orange?

Three hours later, it's time for a snack. Will you have some string cheese? What about lunch? Will you join a friend for sushi and soup? Three hours later it's time for another snack. What'll it be? A handful of nuts or maybe a pudding cup? Three hours later, you've got a dinner date. Decide which veggies will fill your plate. What else will you have? And then of course, you have a special treat, possibly a Hershey's Kiss. Remember, food is fuel and your body feels so great when you give it what it needs.

Level 3
Tuesday

"The minute you start talking about what you are going to do if you lose, you have lost."

—George Shultz

jorge's power thought

Have you ever watched a child eat? They eat a bite, squirm about as they chew it, and of course, play with their food. Plus, they always stop when they've had enough. Is there something we can learn here? You bet! Children listen to the instinctual cues that their bodies send them, so they stop when they're full. If you pay close attention while you eat, you'll notice that the pleasure you get from food tends to diminish as you continue to eat. This is a sign that your body has had enough, but many people eat so fast that they don't notice this signal. *Bring your inner child to the table*. Go ahead and have fun with your food when nobody's looking, and make it last. Make train tracks with your fork in your mashed potatoes; eat your sandwich crust first to make a funny shape. Your dinner will be a lot more fun and you'll probably eat a lot less.

"The more slowly you eat and the more you chew your food, the more likely you'll stop eating before it's too late."

8 minute moves®
upper-body day

MOVE 1: push-up
chest

a. Kneel with your palms on the floor under your chest. Extend one leg and then the other, so that your body weight is balanced on the balls of your feet and your palms. (You can do push-ups with your knees bent if you are not yet ready for standard push-ups.) Your fingers should be pointing forward and your toes pointing down.

b. Keep your back straight as you inhale, bend your elbows, and lower your torso toward the floor. Stop once your elbows are even with your shoulders. Exhale and push up to the starting position. Repeat for up to 1 minute, then proceed to Move 2.

a

b

8-MINUTE LOG				
exercise	move 1	move 2	move 3	move 4
sets				
reps				

MOVE 2: yoga down dog
upper back

a. Kneel on all fours. Lower your hips to your heels and reach your palms as far forward as you can while still keeping your palms against the floor.

b. Exhale as you lift your buttocks toward the ceiling, bringing your body into a V shape. Press your palms into the floor as you lower your chest toward the floor and lift your tailbone toward the ceiling. Breathe normally as you hold for 1 minute. Return to the starting position, then proceed to Move 3 on page 288.

a

b

exercise sequence

1. warm up Jog or march in place for 1 minute.

2. cruise moves Do one 60-second repetition of each of your 4 Cruise Moves. Repeat this cycle and you will be done in 8 minutes.

3. cool down After your Cruise Moves, do these stretches (see page 194).

Sky-reaching pose | Hurdler's stretch | Cobra stretch

upper-body day (cont'd)

MOVE 3: low hover
triceps

a. From the down dog position, lower your hips until you're in a push-up position with your hands under your shoulders.

b. Slowly bend your elbows and lower your torso toward the floor, keeping your elbows close to your body. Stop 1 to 2 inches above the floor. Hold and "hover" for up to 60 seconds as you breathe normally. Release and proceed to Move 4.

a

b

eat nutritionally, *not* emotionally® visualization

Today you will again use the power of visualization to help fuel healthy eating choices. Today you're going to prepare a delicious salad made with vegetables you've grown yourself in your very own garden. Today's visualization will make it possible!

Close your eyes and take a few relaxing breaths, in through your nose and out through your mouth. Allow each exhalation to bring you to a state of deep relaxation. Once you feel completely relaxed, you're ready to begin.

MOVE 4: "show off my muscle" hold
biceps

a. Sit or stand. Firm your abdominals, lengthen and straighten your back, and relax your shoulders. Raise your arms out to the sides, with your palms facing up. Curl your hands in loose fists toward your shoulders. Once in position, show off those muscles! Firm and flex your biceps (the muscles along the upper front of your arms) and hold for 60 seconds, breathing normally. Release, then return to Move 1 on page 286. Repeat Moves 1–4 once more, and you're done.

a

your inner garden

You've just returned from your local garden center with everything you need to start your garden—soil, seeds, transplants, shovel, hoe, watering can, and gloves. You slip on a pair of overalls, put on some sunscreen, and place a wide-brimmed hat on your head

Feel the sun warm your cheeks as you start hoeing the soil. Your arms are strong and firm. As you dig in the soil and plant each seed or transplant, concentrate on how strong your body feels. You treat the garden with gentle care, giving it the nutrients it needs to grow! Picture how the garden will look in a few weeks and then in a month. Imagine the vegetables growing ripe and delicious.

Level 3
Wednesday

"If you think you can, or you think you can't, you're probably right."

—Mark Twain

jorge's power thought

One of the best ways to pamper yourself is with a massage. Whether you pay a professional or get a massage from a loved one, it has the same effect. The motion of the massage helps to increase circulation to your muscles as well as break up any knots or tense spots. This helps your muscles to recover from your Cruise Moves and prevents soreness.

But massage does even more. New research shows that your metabolism gets a boost when you get a massage. So, while you are relaxing on the table, you'll burn up some extra calories without lifting a finger! Also, there's nothing like the sensation of warm touch to help you relax and release all of your emotional worries. Indeed, regular massages are good for mind, body, and soul. Treat yourself to one today. You've earned it!

"Getting a massage is one of the best gifts you can give your body."

8 minute moves®
thighs day

MOVE 1: reclined pillow squeeze
inner thighs

a. Lie on your back with your knees bent and your feet on the floor. Place a thick, firm pillow between your thighs.

b. Exhale as you lift your hips, balancing your body weight on your upper back and feet. Squeeze the pillow between your thighs as if you were trying to squeeze the stuffing out of it. Hold for 40 to 60 seconds as you breathe normally. Release and proceed to Move 2.

a

b

8-MINUTE LOG				
exercise	move 1	move 2	move 3	move 4
sets				
reps				

MOVE 2: doggie hold
outer thighs and hips

a. Kneel on your hands and knees. Make sure your hands are under your shoulders and your knees are under your hips.

b. Keeping your leg bent at a 90-degree angle, exhale as you lift your right leg out to the side (like a dog at a fire hydrant). Hold for 30 seconds. Lower and repeat with the other leg, then proceed to Move 3 on page 294.

a

b

exercise sequence

1. warm up Jog or march in place for 1 minute.

2. cruise moves Do one 60-second repetition of each of your 4 Cruise Moves. Repeat this cycle and you will be done in 8 minutes.

3. cool down After your Cruise Moves, do these stretches (see page 194).

Sky-reaching pose | Hurdler's stretch | Cobra stretch

thighs day (cont'd)

MOVE 3: seated leg lift
fronts of the thighs

a. Sit on the floor with your left leg bent and your right leg extended. Wrap your hands around your left knee for support. Sit with your back long and straight. Try not to slouch.

b. Exhale as you lift your extended right leg as high as you can. Hold for 30 seconds while you breathe normally. Lower and repeat with the other leg, then proceed to Move 4.

a

b

eat nutritionally, *not* emotionally® visualization

Today you will again use the power of visualization to help fuel healthy eating choices. Today is your good friend's birthday and you've invited her over for a healthy and delicious gourmet dinner. Are you ready to get cooking? Close your eyes and take a few relaxing breaths, in through your nose and out through your mouth. Allow each exhalation to bring you to a state of deep relaxation. Once you feel completely relaxed, you're ready to begin.

MOVE 4: kneeling leg lift
backs of the thighs and rear end

a. Kneel on the floor with your hands under your shoulders and your knees under your hips.

b. Exhale as you extend and lift your right leg slightly higher than your torso. Hold for 30 seconds. Release and repeat with your left leg, then return to Move 1 on page 292. Repeat Moves 1–4 once more, and you're done.

a

b

a gourmet meal

You carefully planned the menu earlier in the week and purchased everything you need. You hear the doorbell ring just as you finish chopping the last few veggies for the salad. See yourself open the door and greet your friend with a big birthday hug. You lead her to the dining table, which you've set with your best dishes. See yourself serving each yummy dish. Enjoy each bite and stop eating when you're satisfied, not overly full.

When dinner is cleared, you dim the lights and bring out the cake. She blows out the candles and you each savor a slice. She gives you a big hug and says, "Thank you so much! This really made me feel special. You are a great friend."

Level 3
Thursday

"*The pessimist sees the difficulty in every opportunity; The optimist, the opportunity in every difficulty.*"

—L. P. Jacks

jorge's power thought

I'm sure you've noticed how much better you feel throughout the day after you do your Cruise Moves in the morning. That's not the half of it. Psychologists and exercise physiologists have found that exercise may actually work as well as drugs for treating depression.

A study done at Duke University recently tested this theory. They recruited 156 men and women age 50 and older who suffered from major depression. One group walked or jogged for 30 minutes 3 days a week, while another group took the antidepressant Zoloft. At the end of 4 months, both groups had improved dramatically. When the researchers checked back 6 months later to see how the people were faring on their own, 38 percent of the Zoloft group had fallen back into depression, but only 8 percent of the exercise group saw their symptoms return.

"Your Cruise Moves can help lift your spirits all day long—making you literally start the day on the right foot."

8 minute moves®
torso and calves day

MOVE 1: half-forward bend
belly

a. Stand with your feet under your hips and your knees slightly bent. Inhale as you raise your arms out to the sides and up overhead. Lengthen your spine and reach the crown of your head toward the ceiling.

b. Exhale as you bend forward from the hips, reaching through your fingertips. Stop once your torso and legs form a 90-degree angle. Reach back through your tailbone and forward through your fingertips and the crown of your head. Hold for up to 60 seconds, breathing normally. Inhale and return to the starting position, then proceed to Move 2.

a

b

8-MINUTE LOG				
exercise	move 1	move 2	move 3	move 4
sets				
reps				

MOVE 2: balancing stick
lower back

a. Stand with your feet under your hips and your hands at your sides. Step 2 feet forward with your right foot, keeping both legs extended. Inhale as you raise your arms overhead.

b. Exhale as you bend forward from the hips and simultaneously raise your extended left leg behind until your left leg, torso, and arms are parallel with the floor. Hold for up to 30 seconds, breathing normally. Release, return to the starting position, and repeat with the other leg. Then proceed to Move 3 on page 300.

a

b

exercise sequence

1. warm up Jog or march in place for 1 minute.

2. cruise moves Do one 60-second repetition of each of your 4 Cruise Moves. Repeat this cycle and you will be done in 8 minutes.

3. cool down After your Cruise Moves, do these stretches (see page 194).

Sky-reaching pose | **Hurdler's stretch** | **Cobra stretch**

torso and calves day (cont'd)

MOVE 3: half-handstand
shoulders

a. Kneel with your back to a wall, both feet against the wall. Place your hands under your chest.

b. Lift one leg and place the ball of the foot against the wall. Do the same with the other foot and then walk your feet up the wall until you can straighten your arms, legs, and back. Your torso should be perpendicular to the floor. Hold for up to 60 seconds. Release, then proceed to Move 4. *Note:* If this move is difficult for you, do it with your feet on the ground.

a

b

eat nutritionally, *not* emotionally®
visualization

Today you will strengthen your motivation to stick with the Cruise Down Plate by visualizing yourself in the future. You will envision a day after you've reached your goal, a day when your hips and thighs are slimmer than you've ever dreamed! Today, you're preparing for a very special date. So, first

relax by closing your eyes and taking a few deep, relaxing breaths, in through your nose and out through your mouth. Allow each exhalation to bring you to a state of deep relaxation. Once you feel completely relaxed, you're ready to begin.

MOVE 4: yoga down dog with leg raise
calves

a. Kneel on all fours. Lower your hips to your heels and reach your palms as far forward as you can while still keeping your palms against the floor.

b. Exhale as you lift your buttocks toward the ceiling, bringing your body into a V shape. Press your palms into the floor as you lower your chest toward the floor and lift your tailbone toward the ceiling.

c. Rise onto the balls of your feet. Shift your body weight onto your right foot. Lift your extended left leg as high as possible. Hold for 30 seconds. Switch legs and repeat, then return to Move 1 on page 298. Repeat Moves 1–4 once more, and you're done.

a

b

c

your first date

See yourself getting ready for your date. Who will be your date for the evening? How do you prepare for your date? See yourself taking a hot bubble bath or splurging on a manicure and facial. Then, pick out a beautiful outfit in the back of your closet, one that you've always loved but refused to wear because of your hips and thighs. Maybe it has a slit high up on the leg. Put it on. See how great your legs look in this outfit! Look in the mirror and twirl around and smile at how slim and healthy you look.

Hear the doorbell ring. Open the door and see your date. Hear your date comment on how lovely you look. What does your date say and how does it make you feel?

Level 3
Friday

"Unless you try to do something beyond what you have already mastered, you will never grow."

—Ralph Waldo Emerson

jorge's power thought

Even if you eat a healthful diet that is rich in vegetables and whole grains, you may still be deficient in many important nutrients. In fact, the *Journal of the American Medical Association* has recently reported that "most people do not consume an optimal amount of all vitamins by diet alone" and that "all adults should take one multivitamin daily."

A multivitamin provides extra insurance that you get all of the vitamins and minerals you need, particularly on those extra busy days when you don't eat as well as you should. Make sure your multivitamin contains roughly 100 percent of the Daily Value for most vitamins and minerals. Note that because calcium is a very bulky mineral, most multivitamins only contain a small amount of it. If you have trouble swallowing pills and capsules, that's no excuse to skip your multi. There are plenty of liquid multivitamins on the market.

"For direct links to some of the best vitamins and supplements available, go to my Web site at www.jorgecruise. com."

8 minute moves®
thighs day

MOVE 1: reclined pillow squeeze
inner thighs

a. Lie on your back with your knees bent and your feet on the floor. Place a thick, firm pillow between your thighs.

b. Exhale as you lift your hips, balancing your body weight on your upper back and feet. Squeeze the pillow between your thighs as if you were trying to squeeze the stuffing out of it. Hold for 40 to 60 seconds as you breathe normally. Release and proceed to Move 2.

a

b

8-MINUTE LOG				
exercise	move 1	move 2	move 3	move 4
sets				
reps				

MOVE 2: doggie hold
outer thighs and hips

a. Kneel on your hands and knees. Make sure your hands are under your shoulders and your knees are under your hips.

b. Keeping your leg bent at a 90-degree angle, exhale as you lift your right leg out to the side (like a dog at a fire hydrant). Hold for 30 seconds. Lower and repeat with the other leg, then proceed to Move 3 on page 306.

a

b

exercise sequence

1. warm up Jog or march in place for 1 minute.

2. cruise moves Do one 60-second repetition of each of your 4 Cruise Moves. Repeat this cycle and you will be done in 8 minutes.

3. cool down After your Cruise Moves, do these stretches (see page 194).

Sky-reaching pose | **Hurdler's stretch** | **Cobra stretch**

thighs day (cont'd)

MOVE 3: seated leg lift
fronts of the thighs

a. Sit on the floor with your left leg bent and your right leg extended. Wrap your hands around your left knee for support. Sit with your back long and straight. Try not to slouch.

b. Exhale as you lift your extended right leg as high as you can. Hold for 30 seconds while you breathe normally. Lower and repeat with the other leg, then proceed to Move 4.

a

b

eat nutritionally, *not* emotionally® visualization

Today we will nurture your inner motivation with a very special visualization exercise. During today's visualization, you will be reunited with an old friend who hasn't seen you for many years. So, close your eyes and take a few relaxing breaths, in through your nose and out through your mouth. Allow each exhalation to bring you to a state of deep relaxation. Once you feel completely relaxed, you're ready to begin.

MOVE 4: kneeling leg lift
backs of the thighs and rear end

a. Kneel on the floor with your hands under your shoulders and your knees under your hips.

b. Exhale as you extend and lift your right leg slightly higher than your torso. Hold for 30 seconds. Release and repeat with your left leg, then return to Move 1 on page 304. Repeat Moves 1–4 once more, and you're done.

a

b

seeing an old friend

See yourself pulling into the parking garage at the airport to pick up your friend. Take a quick look in the rearview mirror and smile at your reflection. You look healthier, happier, and younger than you have in years! You have only a few minutes until your friend's flight is due at the gate, so you quickly head to the stairs and mount them two at a time. Feel how agile and strong your body feels as you quickly climb each staircase. You make it just in time to see your friend approach. She smiles politely, says, "Excuse me," and brushes past you. She doesn't recognize you! You call her name and say, "It's me!" Your friend turns around stunned and says, "You look incredible! What have you done?" You smile radiantly.

Level 3
Saturday

"*Hard work won't
guarantee you a
thing, but without
it, you don't stand
a chance.*"

—Patrick Riley

jorge's power thought

Eggs have gotten a bad reputation over the last few decades because health experts thought that eggs raised blood cholesterol levels. In the last few years, numerous health organizations have been vindicating eggs' reputation.

The key is just to use the whites of the eggs. That's where all the protein is that your muscles need in order to grow. The saturated fat in an egg is in the yolk, so I suggest you just eat the protein-rich egg white or try an egg substitute product like Egg Beaters.

Start your day right by making an egg white omelette with lots of veggies. One of my favorite omelettes: chopped spinach, chopped peppers, chopped cooked soy sausage patties, chopped tomatoes, and a carton of egg substitute. Visit JorgeCruise.com for more recipe ideas.

"Some egg substitutes are pasteurized, meaning they're safe to eat without cooking. I use them as the base in smoothies to add more appetite-suppressing protein."

stretches
day off from cruise moves

Today is your day off from your Cruise Moves. To accelerate your results, I suggest that you spend 8 minutes this morning stretching and lengthening your muscles.

STRETCH 1: kneeling thigh stretch
fronts of the thighs

a. Kneel on your hands and knees with your back to a wall. Lift your left knee, placing your left shin and foot against the wall.

b. Lift your right knee, bringing your right foot onto the floor into a modified lunge position.

c. To increase the stretch, lift your torso, placing your hands on your right thigh. The closer you bring your back toward the wall, the more intense the stretch will become. Hold for 30 seconds, breathing normally. Release and then repeat with the other leg. Then proceed to Stretch 2.

eat nutritionally, *not* emotionally®
visualization

Sometimes during the course of a day, we tend to focus only on the negative. We forget all of the good things. When we focus only on the negative, we allow negative emotions such as sadness, guilt, and anger to build out of proportion to reality.

And when that happens, we run to the refrigerator! Today's visualization will help you keep negative emotions in check with reality. Start by taking a few deep, relaxing breaths. Once you feel completely relaxed, you are ready to begin.

STRETCH 2: pigeon yoga stretch
outer thighs and hips

a. Start in a table position with your hands under your chest and your knees under your hips. Lift your left knee and draw it as far forward between your arms as possible. Externally rotate your left thigh, resting your outer left thigh near your left hand and your left heel near your right hip, with the toes pointing to the right. Reach back with your right leg, extending it and placing the top of your right foot on the floor. Keep the sides of your hips even and parallel to the floor.

b. To increase the stretch, reach forward with your hands, resting your torso on your left inner thigh. Hold for 30 seconds, breathing normally. Release and switch legs, then proceed to Stretch 3 on page 312.

cultivating gratitude

Visualize your entire day yesterday. Call to mind every good thing that happened during the entire 24-hour period. Remember every compliment. Remember the traffic lights that were green instead of red. Remember the luck of finding the prime parking space. Recall any instances when someone treated you kindly. Recall any simple pleasures that you experienced, such as the smell of blooming spring flowers or the sight of a rare bird. Take a few more moments to reflect on every good thing that took place yesterday. As you do so, feel your gratitude growing and growing.

stretches
day off from cruise moves (cont'd)

STRETCH 3: seated forward bend
backs of the thighs

a. Sit with your legs extended and your hands at your sides. Inhale as you raise your arms overhead.

b. Exhale as you bend forward, keeping your spine long and straight. Lower your arms to your ankles or shins. Hold and breathe normally for 60 seconds, then release and proceed to Stretch 4.

STRETCH 4: butterfly stretch
inner thighs

a. Sit on the floor. Bend your legs and bring the outer edges of your feet together. Release your knees out to the sides. Grasp your ankles with your hands.

b. Exhale as you lean forward from the hips. Try to keep your spine long and straight. Hold for 60 seconds as you breathe normally. Inhale and rise to the starting position, then return to Stretch 1 on page 310. Repeat Stretches 1–4 once more, and you're done.

Level 3
Sunday

"Look at a day when you are supremely satisfied at the end. It's not a day when you lounge around doing nothing. It's when you've had everything to do, and you've done it."

—Margaret Thatcher

jorge's power thought

Water is so important to your success. Your body is made up of 75 percent water. Your body needs water to create a fluid blood volume. When you become dehydrated, your blood becomes viscous and sticky, making it harder for your heart to pump it through your body. This raises your heart rate, making you feel overly tired during simple movements like your Cruise Moves. Worse, your brain can't distinguish between dehydration and starvation, and responds to both by emitting hunger signals. This means that even though your body is not in need of food, you will feel fatigued, restless, and hungry, when all you really need is a tall glass of water. So instead of getting mixed signals from your body, just give it what it needs: lots of water.

I like to drink a tall glass of water first thing in the morning, right before I do my Cruise Moves. I find that it helps energize me.

"Whenever you feel tired, drink a glass of water. You may really only be dehydrated."

capture your progress
day off from cruise moves

Today is your day off. Take a moment to relish your progress. Grab a pen and answer the following questions. Then share the answers with me by sending an e-mail to thinthighs3@jorgecruise.com.

1. What is your current weight?

_____

2. What was your original weight?

_____

3. What is your waist circumference in inches?

_____

4. What was your original waist circumference in inches?

_____

5. What have you done well this week? What are you most proud of?

_____

_____

_____

_____

_____

6. What could you improve next week?

_____

_____

_____

_____

_____

eat nutritionally, *not* emotionally®
visualization

Sometimes our zeal to control situations is what gets us into trouble emotionally. Today's visualization will help you set aside your problems, allowing yourself to love your life, no matter how it presents itself to you. Start by taking a few moments to relax. Take a few deep breaths, in through your nose and out through your mouth, using your exhalations to bring you to a deeper and deeper state of relaxation. Once you feel deeply relaxed, you are ready to begin.

bonnie barrett lost 4 inches from her thighs!

"Jorge's program has been great for me, and I am so proud of what I have accomplished. I've lost a total of 33 pounds. My thighs have firmed and my bottom has lifted. For the first time in many, many years I bought a pair of shorts. I also recently had fun trying on bathing suits. Clothes shopping is now an awesome experience. I even recently fit into a darling pair of hip-hugger jeans. I was a kid when I last wore that style of jeans, and now I am finally donning them again and getting so many compliments.

"The results are fantastic. My thighs have always been a trouble zone for me, and now I have the tools to zap them! Because the program is so simple and needs so little equipment, it's easy to make it a priority in my life.

I now feel that I have control over eating and my life. I am choosing to live a healthy lifestyle. This program has added years to my life as well as taken years off my appearance. I look and feel so much younger than the day I started the program."

Bonnie went from a size 12 to a size 6.

letting go

Ponder a problem that you are having. Perhaps you are experiencing conflict with your children or maybe you worry about your spouse's frequent late nights at work. Pick just one situation that tends to make you feel at the end of your rope—one to which you see no active solution. Imagine that you are holding your problem in the palms of your hands. Imagine a hope chest in the room. Carry your problem over to the hope chest. Open the lid and carefully place your problem in the bottom of the chest for safekeeping. Close the lid and walk away. Notice how free you feel when you relieve yourself of the need to control or worry about a problem that you can't solve!

Part 4

Bonus Chapters

Chapter 8

Additional Flat Belly Secrets

cleanse your body of false fat!

So far, I've provided you with a simple two-step process for shedding belly fat. Your first step—8 minutes of Cruise Moves—helped you to create the muscle needed to burn the fat. Your second step—Eat Nutritionally, *Not* Emotionally—helped you to further support lean muscle growth and avoid emotional eating.

> "Never give up, surrender, or quit."

This chapter will provide you with some additional secrets that will help accelerate your success. Follow these tips and you'll meet your goal more quickly. You'll also create more energy and feel better from head to toe.

getting rid of false fat

If you are seeking to create a completely flat belly for a special occasion such as a wedding or reunion, you can't ignore what I call false fat.

What is false fat? Let me explain. Sometimes people tell me that no matter what they do, their belly still has a bulge. Usually this bulge isn't from fat. It comes from air, fluid, or wastes causing the intestines to swell. Your large and small intestines are a whopping 25 feet long. When they fail to push your digested food through efficiently, things get backed up, much like a traffic jam. When that happens, your intestines swell and your belly expands.

I've already given you the most important secret for shedding such false fat: your weekly body cleanse. That, along with the extra fiber you'll consume by following the Cruise Down Plate, will help keep your intestinal contents on the move, preventing the logjams that can lead to bloating and belly bulging.

Indeed, bumping up your fiber consumption is your most important weapon against false

your "8 minute" edge

The extra fiber from your Cruise Down Plate, along with your weekly cleansing ritual on Saturdays, will:

- Reduce bloating and gas
- Bolster intestinal health
- Help accelerate your success

fat. Fiber literally adds bulk to your food, helping your food to travel smoothly through your intestinal tract. This not only makes you regular but also reduces bloating! Extra fiber also helps lower cholesterol, reduces hunger, and keeps blood sugar levels steady.

Finally, eating a large amount of fiber will help keep yeast and fungal infections in check. I know some women seem to chronically get a fungal infection called *candida*, which can also cause bloating.

When you bump up your fiber consumption, do so gradually. Your stomach and intestines will need time to adjust to the new fiber load. As you eat more and more fiber, your intestinal tract will learn to secrete more of the right digestive enzymes needed to break it down for digestion. So be patient and go slowly.

tips for body cleansing

During each Saturday of your *8 Minutes in the Morning for a Perfect Body* program, I suggested you cleanse your body with three simple steps:

1. Starting the day with a psyllium shake

2. Drinking eight 16-ounce glasses of water

3. Eating no animal protein at lunch and dinner

Many people don't realize that protein exists in many foods beyond animal products. Many vegetarian foods contain good, quality protein that your muscles need to grow and repair themselves. As an added bonus, they also offer fiber—important for keeping your digestive tract running smoothly. Beans and soy products rank highest on the list for vegetable protein sources. But some whole grains also contain high amounts of protein, too. Here are some examples of vegetable protein meals that you can eat for lunch or dinner on Saturdays.

1. "Sausage" sandwich: One Boca Meatless Italian Sausage on a whole-grain roll with mustard and served with steamed broccoli

2. Fajitas: Heartland Fields Soy Steak Tips sautéed with barbecue sauce and mixed with microwaved chopped onions and peppers, served on a whole-grain tortilla

3. "Chicken" fingers: Morning Star Farms Buffalo Wings served with vegetable soup and a slice of whole-grain bread topped with hummus

4. "Meatball" sandwich: Gardenburger Meatless Meat-balls served in a whole-grain roll with tomato sauce and a slice of melted Veggie Slice soy mozzarella cheese and a side salad

5. Sushi: An appetizer of edamame (steamed soybeans) followed with vegetarian sushi

6. Tofu stir-fry: Slice extra-firm tofu and brown for 10 minutes in olive oil over medium heat, then add any flavoring and mixed frozen vegetables

7. Pizza: Homemade whole-grain dough topped with tomato sauce, Morning Star Farms Breakfast Patties (crumbled), LightLife Smart Deli soy pepperoni, mozzarella cheese, and chopped onions and peppers

8. Beans and rice: Brown rice mixed with onions, peppers, and black beans

9. Soup and salad: Serving of black bean soup, a mixed green salad, and a slice of whole-grain bread dipped in olive oil

10. Frozen vegetarian meals: Any of Amy's frozen entrees, especially the bean enchilada and vegetarian lasagna

additional secrets

Here are some other things you can do to help shed false fat.

Practice positive germ warfare. At any given moment, a number of different types of bacteria—both good and bad—live in your intestinal tract. Usually the different types of bacteria keep each other in check, so no bad bacteria can multiply unchecked. However, certain things, such as the use of antibiotics, can wipe out the friendly bacteria, leaving the unfriendliness to multiply. When this happens, you often feel gassy and bloated. It can also lead to yeast infections.

You can avoid an overpopulation of bad bacteria by eating foods and taking supplements that will replenish your populations of healthy bacteria. Yogurt is a great example of a food that contains friendly bacteria. Look for yogurt that lists "live and active cultures" on the label. You can also take supplements, sold at health food stores under the names *Lactobacilli*, *Bifidobacteria*, and *Acidophilus*.

Check for food sensitivities. Certain foods have been known to cause bloating in certain people. If you have a chronic problem with bloating, cut wheat and dairy foods out of your diet for a week and then add them back in one at a time. If you feel better after you cut these foods out of your diet and worse once you add them back in, you could have a food sensitivity.

Experts say that wheat is among the seven most allergenic foods. It contains two proteins, gluten and glidian, and you may be sensitive to one or both. If you are allergic to wheat, you don't have to give up your favorite carbohydrate foods. A number of manufacturers now sell gluten-free pasta, bread, and other products traditionally made from wheat. As an added bonus, many of these products are made from power whole grains such as quinoa and millet, which are extremely good for your health and waistline!

As for dairy, particularly cow's milk, it, too, can be highly allergenic to certain people. If you're lactose intolerant, you lack a crucial enzyme needed to break down milk and digest it. In addition to avoiding milk and milk products, you also need to read labels, as a milk byproduct called casein is now being used increasingly as a binding agent in many processed foods. If you worry about whether you can get enough calcium without milk, you can. Just take a supplement once a day and drink calcium-fortified juice.

Watch for common offenders. Certain foods tend to irritate the digestive tract, particularly if you have a condition called irritable bowel syndrome or colitis. Highly acidic foods such as tropical and citrus fruits and tomatoes and tomato products can be very irritating for some people. Eat enough of them and you become gassy and bloated. Caffeine can also be irritating. So can chocolate. This doesn't mean that you must completely cut these foods out of your diet. However, you will probably need to cut back. Take a look at your diet and notice how many of these top offenders you tend to eat. If you have an acidic food at every meal—orange juice at breakfast, tomato juice at lunch, tomato sauce at dinner—try to cut back to just one acidic food a day. With a little experimentation, you can still have the foods you love without your digestive tract revolting at the prospect.

Get Longer,
Leaner Legs <u>Even</u>
Faster

three ways to accelerate your results

My Cruise Moves and eating plan will help you build long, sleek muscles that will help burn 2 pounds of fat a week. You'll consistently shrink the size of your belly and hips and thighs by boosting your metabolism.

So far, I've provided you with a simple 2-step process for shrinking the size of your belly and hips and thighs. Your first step—8 minutes of Cruise Moves—helped you to build the muscle needed to burn the fat. Your second step—Eat Nutritionally, *Not* Emotionally—helped to further support lean muscle growth and avoid emotional eating.

That's all you need to see results. However, I know some of you are anxious to see results even faster. I know some of you want to be slimmer *yesterday*. That's where this bonus chapter comes in. This chapter will provide you with some additional secrets that will help accelerate your success. Follow the tips in the bonus chapters and you will meet your goal more quickly. You'll also create more energy and feel better from head to toe.

"No matter when you do it, it's best to stretch when your muscles are warm."

your "8 minute" edge

The three bonus tips in this chapter will help you to:

• Elongate your leg muscles

• Reduce the appearance of cellulite

• Help prevent varicose veins

• Accelerate your results

lengthen your muscles with regular stretching

In chapters 4 and 6, I suggested you use your 8 minutes of free time on Saturdays to your advantage by doing a simple, 8-minute stretching routine. And in the programs on pages 57 and 194, you found some of my favorite stretches for the the belly and hips and thighs.

I'm a firm believer in the power of stretching, particularly when it comes to slimming the belly and hips and thighs area. I've seen firsthand how a regular stretching routine helped my sister, Marta, create longer, leaner, sexier legs. I've also seen the results over and over in my clients.

And there's solid science to back up the powers of stretching. I've already told you that a stretching routine will help to lengthen your muscles. Regular stretching also helps improve circulation, which is important in helping your muscles to recover from your weekly Cruise Moves sessions. Also, stretching improves the health of your connective tissue, helping to prevent those little pockets of fat from bulging through and creating cellulite. Finally, stretching helps to improve your range of motion and flexibility, which, in turn,

help keep your muscles healthy.

Each Saturday, I suggested four 8-minute stretches for you to try. To accelerate your results even more, consider doing my suggested stretching routines every day or every other day. No matter when you do it, it's best to stretch when your muscles are warm. So do these stretches *after* your Cruise Moves, not before. If you don't have more than 8 minutes in the morning, you can also complete your stretching routine just before bedtime, when your muscles are already warm and pliable from moving around all day. In addition to accelerating your results, you'll also help to ready your body and mind for sleep. Many of my clients tell me that a short, pre-bedtime stretching routine helps them to fall asleep faster and sleep more deeply.

When you stretch, always exhale as you move your body into the stretch. Then hold the stretch for 30 to 60 seconds as you breathe normally. Research

has shown that 30 seconds is the minimum amount of time needed for a muscle to lengthen. If you hold the stretch for a shorter amount of time, you won't see results.

Try not to bounce while you stretch, as this can lead to injury. Also, if you feel especially tight in a particular muscle, it sometimes helps to visualize exhaling your breath through the tight muscle. This simple visualization helps coax your muscle to release, allowing you to stretch a bit longer.

improve circulation with regular massage

I often suggest that my clients reward themselves whenever they reach a goal. Some will reward themselves with a new outfit. Others reward themselves by taking a warm, luxurious bath. And some reward themselves with a trip to their local day spa.

Don't forget to stretch

Remember to do your stretches during each week of your *8 Minutes in the Morning for a Perfect Body* program! Your stretches for Level 1 are found on pages 68–99, your stretches for Level 2 are found on pages 100–137, and your

stretches for Level 3 are found on pages 138–175. Remember, it's so important to stretch during this program—it will help you create long, sleek hip and thigh muscles, and will let you see those sexy muscles even *faster*!

If you reward yourself with a massage at your local spa, you'll reap some unexpected bonuses. Massage can do much more than help you to relax and feel pampered. Like stretching, massage also can help lengthen your muscles, creating a longer, leaner appearance. Massage also increases circulation to your muscles, helping them to recover faster from your Cruise Moves.

"Massage increases circulation to your muscles, helping them to recover faster."

And new research shows that massage can also boost your metabolism. No other form of pampering gives you more bang for your buck!

There are many different types of massage. Swedish massage, the most popular type offered at day spas, involves long, light, relaxing strokes. If you're looking for a deeper touch, consider sports, deep muscle, or neuromuscular massage. In those types of massage, the therapist will dig his or her fingers, fists, and elbows deep into your muscles. This helps to break up knots, but also results in some discomfort during the massage.

I often encourage my married clients to take couples massage courses, often offered at local community colleges. Not only does this help you bond and grow closer, it also provides a convenient and affordable way to reap the benefits of massage at home. Here are a few tips for coupling up:

Use cream or some other type of lubricant. This will allow your hands to glide and prevent you from chaffing each other's skin or accidentally yanking out fine body hairs.

Trim your nails. This will prevent accidental pinching and scratching.

Use firm, long strokes. For example, to massage the back of your partner's thigh, place the palm of your hand firmly against his or her thigh and then smoothly move your hand up his or her leg without stopping.

Start with your palms. Use the palms of your hands first. This will help warm up your partner's muscles. Then after a few long, even strokes with your palms, you can provide deeper and more specific pressure with your thumbs.

Communicate. Know that everyone's pain threshold is a little different. You might like very deep pressure, whereas your partner may desire a much lighter touch. As you massage one another, communicate with each other. There's a fine line between "hurts so good" and "hurts like heck." Make sure your partner knows where that line is. If you gently prompt your partner when to go deeper and when to back off, you'll enjoy your massage much more.

reverse gravity to reduce swelling

Your heart has no trouble pumping blood down your legs and to your feet. That's because gravity lends a helping hand. However, once blood gets to your feet, it must make its way back up your legs, against the pull of gravity, and this is where things can go awry.

The force of gravity is one of the main culprits of varicose veins. As blood tries to make its way back up your legs, gravity pulls it downward. If your heart doesn't beat strongly enough or the tiny muscles in your veins fail to effectively push blood upward, it can pool backward, enlarging the size of your veins.

You can do something about this and it's actually a very simple remedy. Every day after work or just before bed, lie on your back and elevate your legs up a wall, as shown, right.

In addition to helping to prevent varicose veins, elevating your legs will help move swelling out of your legs and feet. This will help reduce the appearance

Legs Up the Wall Pose
Elevating your legs helps increase circulation, reduce swelling, and prevent varicose veins.

of cellulite and give your thighs a smoother, sleeker appearance.

It also *feels* really good, particularly if your legs or feet are sore or tired. Make sure to do it any day you spend a lot of time on your feet. Your body will thank you!

the synergy pages

additional jorge cruise tools

Ready for more? Check out these synergistic ways to take the Jorge Cruise weight-control plan to the next level.

jorgecruise.com: the #1 online weight-control club for busy people

Staying motivated can get complicated sometimes. It can be tough tackling everything on your own. As one of my online clients you will have direct access to me and my LIVE coaches to ensure you lose 2 pounds a week in 8 minutes. Having this kind of support can be the difference between reaching the finish line and running in place.

top 7 reasons to join:

1. Accountability: Get daily encouragement directly from me.

2. Accelerate Results: Experience daily LIVE coaching from my personally trained coaches to help maximize your 8-minute workouts and meal planning.

3. End Self-Sabotage: Join daily virtual meetings hosted by my 8-minute mentors who have overcome emotional eating.

4. Find Buddies: 24/7 motivation and support in our Empowerment Circle.

5. Exclusive Tools: Chart your weight loss with our specialized online tools.

6. The Latest 8 Minute Secrets: Attend LIVE auditoriums with me and all other members too!

7. Feel Motivated: As my gift to you, each time you lose 5 pounds you will receive from me via the mail a very special acknowledgment . . . my "Red Rose Magnet" to help you celebrate your success and keep you losing!

Joining our club is like joining a family.

the book series

Build your Jorge Cruise book collection and get all of my secrets to further help you lose up to 2 pounds a week in just 8 minutes! The current full collection includes:

- *8 Minutes in the Morning*
- *8 Minutes in the Morning for Real Shapes, Real Sizes*
- *8 Minutes in the Morning to a Flat Belly*
- *8 Minutes in the Morning to Lean Hips and Thin Thighs*

All these are available in book and in audio kit format. Visit www.jorgecruise.com for full details and all international editions.

the video system

Personally experience my dynamic coaching style in your own home!

With this high-energy video, you will feel that you are shoulder to shoulder with me, your weight-loss coach. I will walk you through, step by step, 1 week's worth of my superquick 8-minute moves. It could not be easier. For more information, go to www.jorgecruise.com system, but look at what my video offers:

• A great companion to this book

• No special equipment required

• Motivating and energetic music to make it more fun

jorge cruise® flax oil

An essential tool to help create your new fat-burning lean muscle tissue!

Flax Oil is an all-natural omega-3 liquid complex that helps control your hunger and tastes great on food. Use as a salad dressing, mixed with yogurt or shakes, on toast in the morning, and much more! Just a teaspoon with each meal, and you will shrink your appetite away. It's also available in capsule form. For more information, go to www.jorgecruise.com, but check out the online shop to purchase flax oil.

Index

Boldface page references indicate photographs. <u>Underscored</u> references indicate boxed text.

about the author

Jorge Cruise: America's #1 Online Weight-Control Specialist

"Time is your most precious commodity. . . . Don't waste it."
—Jorge Cruise

Jorge Cruise struggled with his weight as a child and young man. Today, he has become the #1 online weight-control specialist for busy people with *over 3 million* clients at JorgeCruise.com and the *New York Times* best-selling author of the *8 Minutes in the Morning* books series.

What sets Jorge Cruise® apart from all other weight-loss brands is his guarantee that you will *lose up to 2 pounds each week in just 8 minutes a day*. His secret lies in a revolutionary two-step philosophy that restores your metabolism by creating new lean muscle. Lean muscle makes you look young, toned, and most important, burns fat 24 hours a day!

Jorge has been featured in the *New York Times*, *USA Today*, *People*, *Woman's World*, *First for Women*, *Self*, *Shape*, *Cosmopolitan*, and *Fit*, and has appeared on *Oprah*, CNN, *Good Morning*

America, *Dateline NBC*, Lifetime TV, and *The View*.

No other weight-loss specialist has had so many people report what really works to consistently lose 2 pounds a week in just 8 minutes each day. This makes Jorge one of the most up-to-date and in-demand weight-loss specialists both online and off-line.

Jorge is also a nominee for Fitness Instructor of the Year by IDEA, the national association of fitness professionals, and was named by Arnold Schwarzenegger as a special advisor to the California Governor's Council on Physical Fitness and Sports. In addition, Jorge is also a member of the Association of Health Care Journalists, a nonprofit organization dedicated to advancing public

understanding of health care issues. He is fluent in both English and Spanish.

Utilizing the knowledge and credentials that he has gained from the University of California, San Diego (UCSD), Dartmouth College, the Cooper Institute for Aerobics Research, the American College of Sports Medicine (ACSM), and the American Council on Exercise (ACE), Jorge is dedicated to helping time-deprived people lose weight and achieve their dreams.

He lives in San Diego with his wife, Heather. He can be contacted via JorgeCruise.com.

Me and my girl, Heather